Copyright © 2013, 2008, 2001, 1997 by PAGODA Academy, Inc.

All rights reserved. No part of this publication may be reproduced, stored in a retrieval system, or transmitted, in any form, or by any means, electronic, mechanical, photocopying, recording or otherwise, without the prior written permission of the copyright holder and the publisher.

Published by Wit&Wisdom
Wit&Wisdom is the professional language publishing company of the
PAGODA Education Group.
19F, PAGODA Tower, 419, Gangnam-daero,
Seocho-gu, Seoul, 06614, Rep. of KOREA
www.pagodabook.com

Imprint | PAGODA Books

First published 2013
Ninth impression 2021
Printed in the Republic of Korea

ISBN 978-89-6281-496-5 (13740)

Publisher | Ruda Go
Writers | Judson Wright, Lee Robinson, Kristin Quackenbush
Editor | Paul Adams
Advisor | Ruda Go
Illustrator | Dae Ho Kim

Acknowledgements
Sang Hee Kang, Song Rim Park, Hana Sakuragi, Stephen Willetts, Ian Windsor, and Gemma Young for their support
Nathan Benzschawel, Christina Bromberg, Chasity Davis, Christina DeMers, Mike Dent, Paul Hershberger, Patrick Farrell, Christopher Jack, Martin Middleton, Donald Nairn, Kat Paterson, Phil Robinson, David Spiegle, Tiara Smith, and Meredith Watson for trialing and feedback
Rich Debourke, Jay Hilalen, Jess Kroll, Gina Oh, Tiara Smith, Stephen Willetts, and Gemma Young for voice recording

A defective book may be exchanged at the store where you purchased it.

To Our Students

The SLE program is a conversation program for adult and young adult students who want to improve their English in an enjoyable, effective, and authentic way. The book allows students to use English in a variety of contexts with an emphasis on different useful functions. Our goal is to improve your confidence in your speaking, listening, reading, and writing ability while improving your vocabulary and grammar skills. We will help you to understand not only the "How" but the "Why" of English usage.

The SLE Level 2 textbook series is meant for students with a very good understanding of the basics of English. The material in this book focuses on building students' ability to perform basic functions and use essential structures.

Contents   SLE Generations 2 Compact

- To Our Students | 3
- Format of the Book | 6
- Goals for the Course | 7
- Meet the Thompson Family | 8

UNIT 1
Getting to Know You

Social Skills at Work and Play
▶ 11

LESSON 1 | 12
LESSON 2 | 16

UNIT 2
Talk is Cheap

Communication
▶ 27

LESSON 1 | 28
LESSON 2 | 34

UNIT 3
There and Back Again

and Transportation
▶ 43

LESSON 1 | 44
LESSON 2 | 52

UNIT 4
A Day in the Life

Day-to-Day Activities
▶ 61

LESSON 1 | 62
LESSON 2 | 68

UNIT 5
Better Safe Than Sorry

Social and Global Problems
▶ 79

LESSON 1 | 80
LESSON 2 | 86

UNIT 6
You Don't Say

Finding Meaning
▶ 97

LESSON 1 | 98
LESSON 2 | 104

Listening Dialogues	220
Glossary	228
Additional Activities	234

UNIT 7
Coulda, Woulda, Shoulda
Past Speculations and Regrets
▶ 117

LESSON 1 | 118
LESSON 2 | 126

UNIT 8
The Future is Now
Future Speculations and Technology
▶ 135

LESSON 1 | 136
LESSON 2 | 144

UNIT 9
Shop Til You Drop
Shopping and Preferences
▶ 153

LESSON 1 | 154
LESSON 2 | 160

UNIT 10
The Art of Conversation
Communication Skills
▶ 169

LESSON 1 | 170
LESSON 2 | 176

UNIT 11
Good Intentions
Success and Failure
▶ 185

LESSON 1 | 186
LESSON 2 | 192

UNIT 12
Make It Up As You Go
Storytelling and Inferences
▶ 203

LESSON 1 | 204
LESSON 2 | 212

Format of the Book:

Overall Format >
There are ten units in this textbook, each with its own focus. In each unit there are two individual lessons. The focus of the lesson is either grammatical or topical. Each unit consists of the following elements:

Warm Up >
The warm up for each lesson has its own purpose. The lesson one warm up is used as an opportunity to start thinking about the topic and includes functional language such as idioms, collocations, and tongue twisters that relate to the topic as a whole. The lesson two warm up is used as a quick review of the language used in the first lesson and a bridge to the second lesson.

WARM UP
Ask your partner a question. up question, and think of ano conversation going.
1. What was the last _____
(Movie/Play/Art Show/Co
How was it?

Listening >
Each listening follows the story of the Thompson family and relates to the unit topic and language points used in that unit. Each listening requires the student to make predictions based on illustrations and use communicative language to discuss what they have heard.

Listening TRACK 4-5
Richard is trying to make plans with his indecisive high school classmate, Stan.
While you're listening, check the person, place, or thing Richard and his friend decide on.

Language Point >
Language points occur at the start of any activity where a specific grammar or function point is used in that activity and needs to be explained to the student.

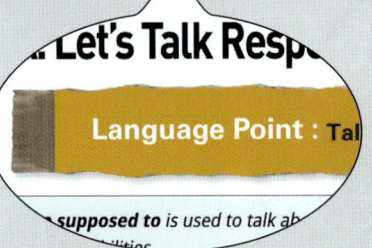

A. The Devil's Debate
Choose one of the opinions below, and simply say whethe you agree or disagree. Your partner(s) MUST disagree with y

Example: It is acceptable for both men and women to stay at home a
A: I believe that it is perfectly acceptable for men to stay at home
B: I disagree. Even if a man is good with children it is really important that a mothe or she is young.

1. It is equally acceptable for men and wo to stay home and take care of c

Activities >
Each lesson consists of a structured activity, a communicative activity, and a task based activity. All units include a "Bonus activity" that can add to the lesson.

BONUS Activity : And the

Discussion Questions >
Each lesson has a short series of discussion questions that relate to the topic and encourage the use of asking follow up questions.

Boxes >
Several boxes are found throughout the text and have different functions:

- **Recycle Box**
Reminds the student of language points they have used previously in SLE.

- **Third Wheel**
Gives a suggestion of how students can perform an activity with an extra student.

- **Do You Know?**
Explains the reason why language is used in a specific way.

- **Do You Remember?**
Reminds students of vocabulary from a previous lesson.

- **Tip**
Gives a tip on how the student can acquire the language easier.

Segue Activity >
The segue activity consists of a reading that relates to the topic of the listening, discussion questions which check the comprehension of the reading, and a short writing task on the topic.

Topics include:

Art, Work, Communication, Change, Adversity, Travel, Daily Routines, Personalities, Celebrations, Well-being, Free Time, Money, Emergencies, Non-verbal Communication, Regrets, Culture, Lifestyles, Technology, Media, Planning, Responsibility, Dilemmas, Shopping, Dreams, Success, Storytelling

Goals for the Course:

1
You should be able to use the following grammatical structures:

- **a** Indirect questions
- **b** Tag questions
- **c** Conditionals (Real and Unreal possibilities)
- **d** Active vs. Passive voice
- **e** Causative passive
- **f** Past speculation using modal verbs
- **g** Contrast using even though and although
- **h** Relative pronouns in adjective clauses
- **i** Future speculation using modal verbs
- **j** Adjective order
- **k** Gerunds when defining concepts

2
You should be able to perform the following functions:

- **a** Understanding when to use formal vs. informal greetings
- **b** Describing Job fields and qualifications
- **c** Giving and receiving advice
- **d** Expressing levels of importance with modal verbs
- **e** Interpreting and using nonverbal communication
- **f** Expressing degrees of certainty in the past tense and future tense
- **g** Talking about regrets
- **h** Discussing resolutions for complex problems
- **i** Talking about clothing and shopping
- **j** Describing and marketing products
- **k** Showing interest during conversation
- **l** Using euphemism, exaggeration, and sentence stress
- **m** Making inferences to fill in missing information

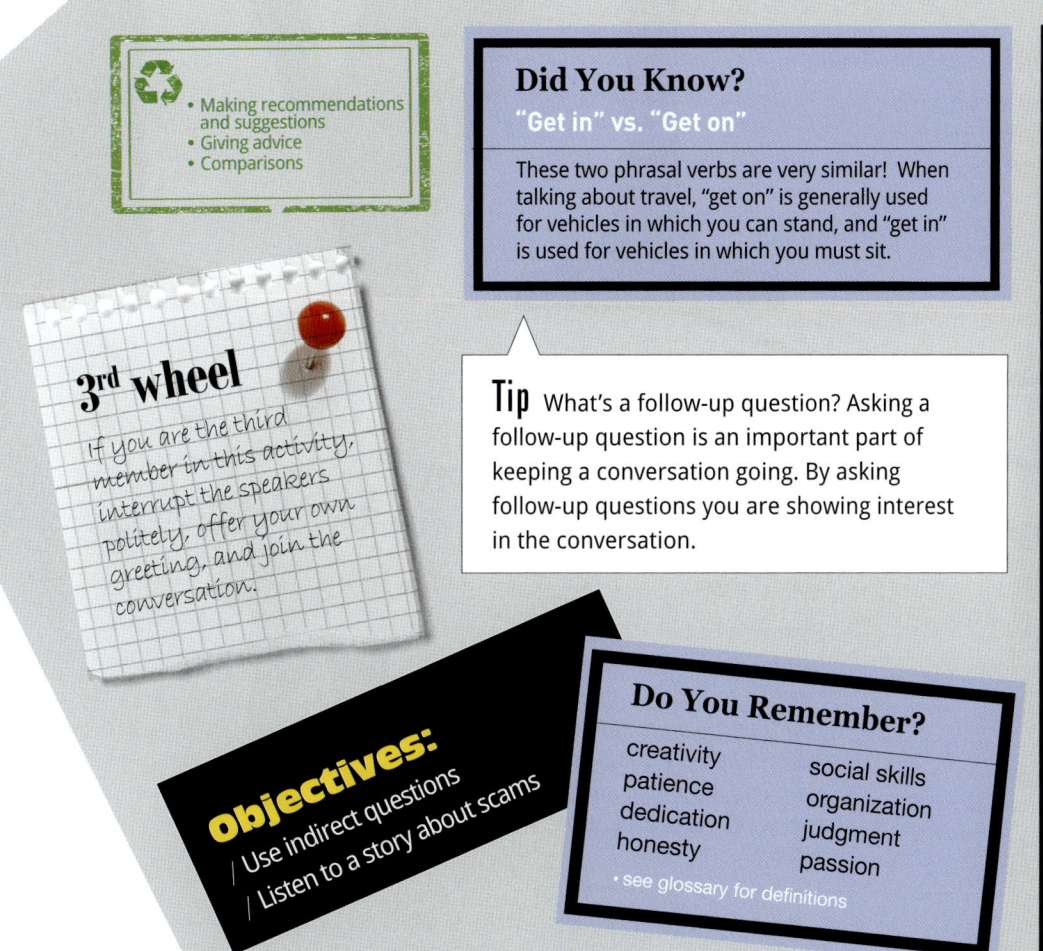

- Making recommendations and suggestions
- Giving advice
- Comparisons

Did You Know?
"Get in" vs. "Get on"

These two phrasal verbs are very similar! When talking about travel, "get on" is generally used for vehicles in which you can stand, and "get in" is used for vehicles in which you must sit.

3rd wheel
If you are the third member in this activity, interrupt the speakers politely, offer your own greeting, and join the conversation.

Tip What's a follow-up question? Asking a follow-up question is an important part of keeping a conversation going. By asking follow-up questions you are showing interest in the conversation.

objectives:
- Use indirect questions
- Listen to a story about scams

Do You Remember?
creativity, patience, dedication, honesty, social skills, organization, judgment, passion
• see glossary for definitions

Need to Know:

• **to be fired**
Lucas **was fired** from his job because he stole money from the safe.

• **to be laid off**
Because of budget cuts, thirty employees **were laid off** last week.

• **to retire**
My parents **retired** when they were 60 years old.

• **to quit**
She **quit** her job because the salary was too low.

• **to get promoted**
When Fred **got promoted**, he received a higher salary.

Meet the Thompson Family
Several of the activities will follow their lives and daily routines.

Jack Thompson

Age: 22
Blood type: A
Job: Senior at University

Jack is a friendly, relaxed young man, though many people think he is very lazy. He enjoys drinking with his friends and listening to his favorite band: the Crimson Kings. He will graduate from university soon and is starting to look for a new job. But not very hard.

Susan Thompson

Age: 42
Blood type: B
Job: Owns a small catering business

Susan is a logical, smart, and independent woman. She loves reading non-fiction, especially biographies. In her free time, Susan enjoys relaxing with an old movie and a large cup of tea.

Baby Jane

Charles Thompson

Age: 67
Blood type: O
Job: Retired

Richard's Father. Charles is an adventurous old man with the heart of a child. He doesn't always consider the consequences of his actions. When he was younger, he joined the military and traveled the world. He enjoys hiking and fishing.

Richard Thompson

Age: 45
Blood type: A
Job: Marketing

Richard is a motivated, hard-working, and creative man. He enjoys spending time with his family. He is an excellent cook. He also reads lots of different newspapers. He is very good at his job, and he recently received a new promotion.

Martha Thompson

Age: 65
Blood type: A
Job: Retired

Richard's Mother. Martha is a kind and quirky old woman, though sometimes she is a little forgetful. She writes poetry and secretly loves watching reality television. She is very concerned about eating healthy food.

Lisa Thompson

Age: 19
Blood type: AB
Job: Freshman at University

Lisa is an ambitious and outgoing young woman, though her ambition sometimes means she gets easily stressed. She graduated high school last year and this is her first year of university. She loves going to the park on sunny days and shopping on rainy days.

Mr. Squiggles

Age: 3
Job: Cat

Mr. Squiggles is the playful family cat. He enjoys eating, scratching furniture, taking naps in Lisa's lap, and chasing Jack around the house. Sometimes, he likes to take Susan's things and hide them under the couch.

Humm... Are You Ready To Meet Them?

WARM UP

Ask the questions below and then ask two follow-up questions to keep the conversation going!

> **Example:**
> **A:** *What's your favorite food?*
> **B:** *Hot dogs!*
> **A:** *Really? Where's the best place to get a hot dog in this city?*
> **B:** *Well... I think it's Hot Diggity Dog......*

> **Tip** What's a follow-up question? Asking a follow-up question is an important part of keeping a conversation going. By asking follow-up questions you are showing interest in the conversation.

1 What is your favorite hobby?
  ▶ Where do you _____?
  ▶ _____?

2 What was the last movie you watched?
  ▶ Did you _____?
  ▶ _____?

3 Do you have any pets?
  ▶ _____?
  ▶ _____?

4 Have you ever lived in another country or traveled abroad?
  ▶ _____?
  ▶ _____?

5 Can you speak any foreign languages besides English?
  ▶ _____?
  ▶ _____?

Unit 1 Getting to Know You | 11

LESSON 1

A. Have You Ever...?

PART 1 ● **Follow these instructions:**

1. Hold up ten fingers.
2. Go through each item on the list below. If you **have** done the action, drop a finger.
3. Discuss some of the things you have done and ask follow-up questions.

Have you ever...

... **skipped** a class in school?
... smoked a cigarette?
... fallen asleep in the movie theatre?
... lied to your parents?
... kissed someone on the first date?
... been bungee jumping?
... dated someone older than you?
... traveled to another country alone?
... cheated on an exam?
... been **engaged**/married?

PART 2 ● **Ask and answer questions using the present perfect.**

Have you ever...?

1. skied in _____?
2. _____?
3. _____?
4. _____?
5. _____?
6. _____?

Do You Remember The Present Perfect?

subject + have/has + past participle

Example:
*I **have seen** that movie already.*
*She **has** never **been** to Hawaii.*

skip school *(idiom)*: to not go to school without permission
engaged *(adj.)*: promised to marry

B. First Day of Work

Tip A prediction is a guess about what you think is going to happen. Making predictions is important because it can help you to understand the listening better.

Pre-listening

Part 1 ● Have you ever been confused for somebody else? Have you ever **mistaken** a stranger for someone you thought you knew? What happened? If this has never happened to you, how do you think you would feel?

Part 2 ● Now look at the picture below. Make predictions about what happened to Richard on his first day of work. What do you think happened to Richard?

Listening TRACK 2-3

Listen to the dialogue to find out what really happened. Do you think the people are speaking formally or informally with each other?

Post-listening

Part 1 ● Discuss what happened in the dialogue. What mistake did Richard make? Was it much different from your original prediction? What happened differently?

Part 2 ● Everybody makes mistakes. What would you do in the following situations?

1. You were very sleepy in the morning. You arrive at work or class and realize that you still have your pajamas on. *I would...*

2. You wrote a very romantic email to the person you are interested in, but instead of sending it to him/her, you accidentally sent it to everyone in your class or office. *I would...*

3. You have to give an important speech in ten minutes. While you are preparing, you accidentally spill coffee all over the front of your clothes. You do not have time to go home and change. *I would...*

mistake *(v.)*: to accidentally think someone is another person

C. You're Fired!

Talk about the following situations. What do you think is going to happen to the employee? What would you do if it were your decision?

> **Example:** During business meetings with the CEO, Grace was checking her email and sending text messages on her new smart phone.
> **A:** *The CEO is probably going to **fire** her. What would you do if you were the boss?*
> **B:** *I would **fire** her because it's really rude to check your phone during meetings.*

1 Bill did not show up to work on Thursday. He said that his grandmother had died. The problem is that he already used that excuse once before.

2 Sue *proposed* a new *budget* for the company which saved them $3.4 million dollars.

3 Pete came into his office early and caught his boss looking through his coworker's personal email.

4 Marge has been with the company for over forty years and is finally thinking about what to do with the rest of her life.

5 Rodrigo has worked very hard at his new job. Even though most of his coworkers do less work, they have been at the company for a long time. Due to the recent economy, the company is not making enough money.

6 Penny is the boss's daughter. She was hired and immediately given a position as a project leader. Within the first two weeks, seven workers made *complaints* about her.

7 Todd and Mindy have been in a relationship for over a month even though it is against company policy for coworkers to date. Todd is Mindy's manager. Someone recently overheard them kissing in the stairwell and is threatening to tell their boss about the relationship.

Need to Know:

- **to be fired**
  Lucas **was fired** from his job because he stole money from the safe.

- **to be laid off**
  Because of budget cuts, thirty employees **were laid off** last week.

- **to retire**
  My parents **retired** when they were sixty years old.

- **to quit**
  She **quit** her job because the salary was too low.

- **to get promoted**
  When Fred **got promoted**, he received a higher salary.

- **to get demoted**
  The head director **got demoted** for poor performance in his department.

---

propose *(v.)*: to make a suggestion
budget *(n.)*: a plan for spending money
complaint *(n.)*: a reason for not being satisfied

Discussion Questions

1 What are some good conversation questions to ask someone you have just met?

2 Do you get nervous when meeting new people?

   ▶ What experiences have you had that felt embarrassing or uncomfortable?

3 What do you think are some good places to meet people?

   ▶ Why do people like to go to these places to socialize?

4 What do you usually talk about with your friends?

   ▶ How about your family or your coworkers?

5 Do you think first impressions are important? Why or why not?

   ▶ What are the first things you notice about a person you have just met?

6 What are the qualities of a good friend?

   ▶ Why do you think so?

7 When people meet new *acquaintances*, they often talk about the weather or what they do for work. What topics do you think are safe or unsafe to talk about with people you don't know very well?

to overcome *(v.)*: to deal with a difficult situation
acquaintance *(n.)*: a person you know

LESSON 2

>> WARM UP

Look at the pictures and answer the following questions for each:

> What is this person's job?
> What are the job requirements?
> Do you think he/she makes good money? What benefits does he/she enjoy?
> Which job do you think is the best? Would you like to have this job? Why or why not?

Remember to ask follow-ups!

Objectives:
/ Talk about job requirements
/ Use informal vs. formal greetings

A. What It Takes

Discuss the kinds of jobs available in each field below. Think of at least two examples for each. Discuss the characteristics they require for success.

Example:
I think a writer needs creativity and determination to do her job. How about you?

Do You Remember?

creativity	social skills
patience	organization
dedication	judgment
honesty	passion

• see glossary for definitions, pg.228

Unit 1 Getting to Know You | **17**

B. Job Interviews

Imagine that you are interviewing applicants for a job at your company. Decide what kind of company it is. Then look at each of the numbered items. Do you think they are important qualities for a candidate? Why or why not?

> **Example:**
> *A: How important is it that Darren has good hair?*
> *B: Well, it's very important if he plans to apply for a management job. What do you think?*

1 Attitude/Self Confidence

2 Appearance
- Hair
- Speaking Ability
- Height
- Weight
- Clothing

Resume

Name : Darren Deeds

3 *Educational Background:*
Bachelor's degree in Economics from the William County College;
Master's degree in Business Administration from Princeton University
GPA: 3.2

4 *Experience:*
Five years tutoring at A-1 Academy

5 *Personal Information:*
Age: 25
Parents: Married 37 years
Blood Type: A
Religion: Roman Catholic
Hobbies: Working out, Playing the guitar, Reading mystery novels

6 *References:*
Economics professor; Former boss

Need to Know

- **degree**
  - Bachelor of Arts (BA)
  - Master of Arts (MA)
  - Doctor of Philosophy (Ph.D.)

- **undergraduate** *(adj.)*

  When I was an **undergraduate** student, I majored in English Literature.

- **graduate** *(adj.)*

  His **graduate** program took three years to complete.

---

reference *(n.)*: a person who can give information about another's ability

C. Good Morning, Sir

Language Point : Formal vs. Informal Greetings
There are different ways of greeting people, depending on the situation.

Example: Formal: *Hello, how are you?*
Informal: *Hey, what's up?*

Formal

A Good morning, sir. How are you?
B I'm doing well, thank you. How are you, Michael?
A I'm fine, thank you.

A Hello Professor Jones, how are you?
B Hi Tom, I'm doing all right, thanks. How about yourself?
A I'm doing well, thanks.

A Hi honey, did you have a good day at school?
B Hi Mom. Yeah, it was OK, I guess.
A Just OK?

Informal

A Hey Sheila, what's up? Want to go see a movie later?
B Yeah, sure! What movie do you want to see?
A Let's go see that new Brad Pitt movie.

Act out the following situations. Greet each other using an informal or formal expression depending on the situation. If the role has (Start) in it you should greet the other person first.

Example:

A: *Good afternoon, miss. How are you today?*
B: *Very well, thank you. What may I help you with?*
C: *Pardon me for interrupting. I just wanted to say thank you for the card.*

STUDENT A

3rd wheel

If you are the third member in this activity, interrupt the speakers politely, offer your own greeting, and join the conversation.

1
Role: You are a university student (Start).
Situation: You have a question about an **upcoming** exam. As you are walking on campus, you see your professor. Greet him and ask the question. Be sure to finish the conversation appropriately.

2
Role: You are a university student.
Situation: You have an important English Literature exam tomorrow morning. Another student missed a class and wants to speak to you. Greet him/her, answer the question(s), and finish the conversation appropriately.

3
Role: You are a Mom/Dad (Start).
Situation: You are **picking up** your son/daughter from middle school at the end of the day. Greet him/her, ask questions about the school day, and finish the conversation appropriately.

4
Role: You are a friend.
Situation: You made plans with a friend to go see a movie. Greet your friend, talk about which movie you want to see, and finish the conversation appropriately.

5
Role: You are a teacher (Start).
Situation: You are meeting with one of your students' parents because the student created a problem in class. Greet the parent, explain the situation, and finish the conversation appropriately.

6
Role: You are a CEO.
Situation: While you are sitting in your office, a new employee stops by to say hello. Greet him/her, ask a few questions, answer his/her questions, and finish the conversation appropriately.

upcoming *(adj.):* happening soon
to pick up *(phrasal v.):* to collect someone or something from a location

STUDENT B

1
Role: You are a university professor.
Situation: While you are walking on campus, one of your students approaches you. Greet him/her and answer the question. Be sure to finish the conversation appropriately.

2
Role: You are a university student (Start).
Situation: You missed your English Literature class this morning. There will be an important exam tomorrow. Greet another student that is in your class, and ask if you can see his/her notes. Finish the conversation appropriately.

3
Role: You are a son/daughter.
Situation: It is the end of the school day and your mother/father has arrived to take you home. Greet him/her, answer the questions, and finish the conversation appropriately.

4
Role: You are a friend (Start).
Situation: You made plans to go see a movie with your friend. Greet him/her, talk about which movie you want to see, and finish the conversation appropriately.

5
Role: You are a parent.
Situation: Your child's teacher wants to meet with you about a problem your child is having in school. Greet him/her, discuss the problem, and conclude the conversation appropriately.

6
Role: You are a company employee (Start).
Situation: It is your first day on the job. As you are walking to your desk, you see your boss in his/her office. Greet the CEO, introduce yourself, answer his/her questions, and finish the conversation appropriately.

Discussion Questions

1. What is your dream job?
   - Why do you think this job would be good for you?
2. When considering a job, what are you most concerned about: job satisfaction or **job security**?
   - Why?
3. Do you think men and women are treated equally in the workplace?
   - Why or why not?
4. Do you think it is fair that employers prefer to hire graduates from **prestigious** universities?
   - Why or why not?
5. If you started your own company, what kind of company would it be?
   - Why?
6. After graduating from university, how important is it to get a job related to your major?
   - Why do you think so?
7. What will you do if you cannot find the job that you want after you graduate?
   - Why will you do this?
8. What is the most boring job in the world?
   - How about the most interesting job? Why do you think so?
   - How about the most dangerous job? Why do you think so?

UNIT 1 REVIEW

How well can you use:
- ☐ Present perfect review: **subject + have/has + past participle**?
- ☐ Formal vs. informal greetings?
- ☐ Job skills and attributes?

What do you need to study more?

job security *(n.)*: the knowledge that an employee will not lose his or her job
prestigious *(adj.)*: having a good reputation

Activity: Downsizing

You and your classmates are supervisors at a company. The CEO has decided to make the company smaller. One of your workers has to be laid off. The qualifications of each worker are listed below. Decide which of these individuals should be let go. After you are finished, discuss your choice with others in the class.

Name	Christie	Roger	Melissa	Don
Age	34	27	21	47
Marital Status	Divorced	Single	Engaged	Married
Dependents	2 children	Mother	None	Wife and 18-year-old son
Education	Vocational high school graduate	High school dropout	College student	Graduate school at night
Health	Used to be an alcoholic; **sober** for 7 years	**Disabled**, but this does not affect his work	Excellent	A little overweight
Seniority	8 years	5 years	2 years	6 years
Other Qualities	Slow worker / gets along well with everyone / sometimes late / a little moody but honest	Good worker / good relationship with coworkers / sometimes late / friendly	Average worker / liked by most coworkers / frequently late / friendly and outgoing	Efficient worker / does not get along well with others / never late / quiet and often **grouchy**
Future	Would like to keep her current position	Hopes to get a promotion in this company	Her uncle is the company CEO	Will probably change jobs when he finishes school

Example:

A: *I think we need to lay off Richard. The boss doesn't really like him after that copy machine incident. What do you think?*

1. Who would your first choice be? Why?
2. Who would your second choice be? Why?
3. Who do you think deserves to keep their job? Why?

sober *(adj.)*: not influenced by alcohol
grouchy *(adj.)*: having a bad temper or being in a bad mood
disabled *(adj.)*: a physical or mental condition that limits a person's ability

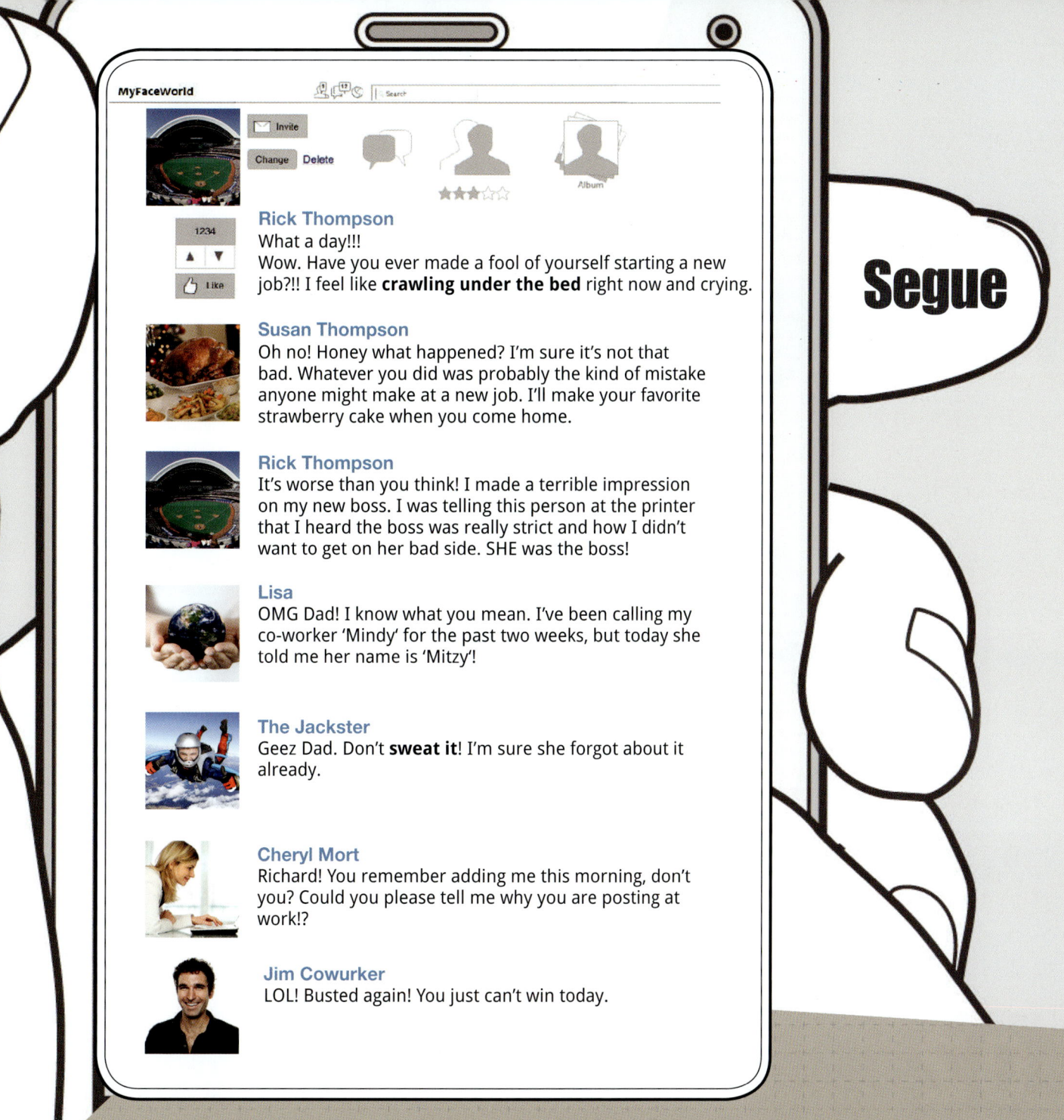

A. Discussion
1. Do you communicate with your friends and family using social network sites? Why or why not?
2. Richard says that he **"feels like crawling under the bed"**. Have you ever been in a situation where you felt like crawling under the bed? What happened?
3. Jack tells Richard not to **"sweat it"** or worry. Do you think Richard is overreacting to the situation?

B. Writing
Write a short response of 4-6 sentences to Richard telling him about a time you were in a similar situation or try to make him feel better about his situation.

02
Talk is Cheap

Communication

Objectives:
/ Use indirect questions
/ Listen to a story about scams

WARM UP

Do you think it is polite to ask the following questions to someone you have just met? Why or why not?

- How old are you?
- Are you married?
- Where do you work?
- What kind of car do you drive?
- What is your religion?
- What's your blood type?
- Do you have children?
- Where did you buy that dress?
- What university did you go to?
- Do you come here often?

COLLOCATIONS

- **say a word**
  He didn't *say a word* about my new haircut.
- **strictly speaking**
  Strictly speaking, a tomato is a fruit and not a vegetable because it has seeds.
- **get the message across**
  His loud voice and serious tone really *got the message across*.
- **conflicting information**
  We're receiving *conflicting information* about who won the race.

IDIOMS

- **loud and clear**
  You don't need to repeat yourself; I got your message *loud and clear*.
- **speak your mind**
  I'm so angry at her! I'm going to call her right now and *speak my mind* about the situation.
- **pour your heart out**
  When we went out to dinner last night, Jim *poured his heart out* about the divorce.
- **My lips are sealed.**
  Don't worry, I won't tell anyone about your money problems. *My lips are sealed*.

TONGUE TWISTER

Red leather, yellow leather. Red leather, yellow leather.
Red leather, yellow leather. Red leather, yellow leather.
Red leather, yellow leather. Red leather, yellow leather.
Red leather, yellow leather. Red leather, yellow leather.

LESSON 1

A. Do You Know...?

Language Point: Indirect Questions

Why do you think the older woman is angry at Lisa?

Indirect questions are often used to be more polite. For example, if you are talking to a stranger, an information question can sound too direct.

Example
Direct: *What time is it?*
Indirect: *Could you tell me **what time it is**?*

◇ Notice the word order is **not** switched like in a direct question.
Also remember:
- Yes/No questions require *if or whether*.
- The auxiliary verb *do* is not used in indirect questions.

Example
Direct question:
Does the express train stop in Springfield?
Indirect question: *Can you tell me if the express train stops in Springfield?*

main questions	indirect question	
Do you know	What	
Can you tell me	Where	
Have you heard	When	
	Who	**subject + verb + object**
main statements	Why	
I don't know	How	
I can't remember		
Please tell me	if (for yes/no)	
I was wondering		

28 | SLE Generations 2 Compact

Discuss the following:

- Identify the indirect question(s) in each dialogue and underline them.
- What is the situation? Where is it taking place?
- What do you think the relationship is between the people?

A: I'm almost finished with all of my homework!
B: Great! I was wondering if you will have time to help me do the laundry.
A: No way. That was my chore last week.

1

A: Hi there. It's Jinny, right?
B: Ya. What can I do for you?
A: I need to find out if there was any homework from our last class.
B: Oh sure. We had to read and respond to the essay on page 32.

2

A: Why did you do it?
B: I don't know what you're talking about! Can you prove I did it? Where is your proof?
A: Don't play games with me. We have witnesses!
B: Oh. In that case... tell me if I can call my lawyer now.

3

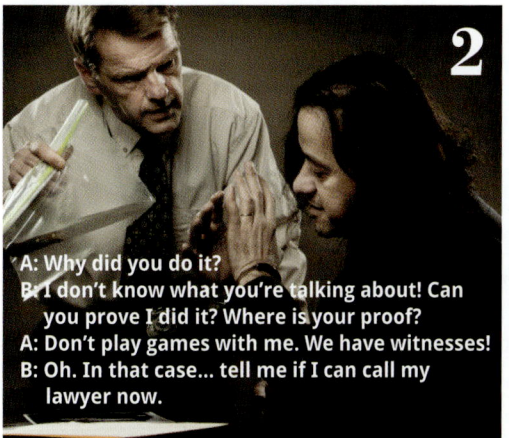

4

A: Reynolds! This is the third time this week. Would you like to tell me why you were late?
B: I'm so sorry, ma'am. The subway wasn't running well.
A: I don't know if I believe that. Peterson takes the same subway and he wasn't late!

5

A: Excuse me, but could you tell me what time it is?
B: Of course. It's half past four.
A: Thanks!
B: No problem.

6

A: Do you have any idea how he did it?
B: I can't remember what he pushed. I think he pushed two buttons on the remote control at the same time.
A: Um, do you know what that **beeping** sound is?
B: Maybe we should call **tech support**.

beep *(n.)*: a sound made by something electronic
tech support *(n.)*: help from people who provide assistance for computers
proof *(n.)*: something that indicates truth
play games *(idiom)*: try to gain an advantage by being dishonest
witness *(n.)*: a person who sees an action in progress

B. The Egyptian Koala

Language Point : Uses of Indirect Questions

Indirect questions can be used to ask questions that sound more polite.

> **Example:**
> **A:** *Would you mind telling me **what your account number is**?*
>
> They can also be used to clarify or confirm information.
> **B:** *Why do you want to know **what my bank account number is**?*
> **A:** *I want to send some money to your account.*
> **B:** *Oh. In that case, I don't mind telling you **what my account information is**.*

Pre-listening

When it comes to getting information, who do you believe? Go through the list of information sources below.

1. Do you think this source of information is trustworthy? Why or why not?

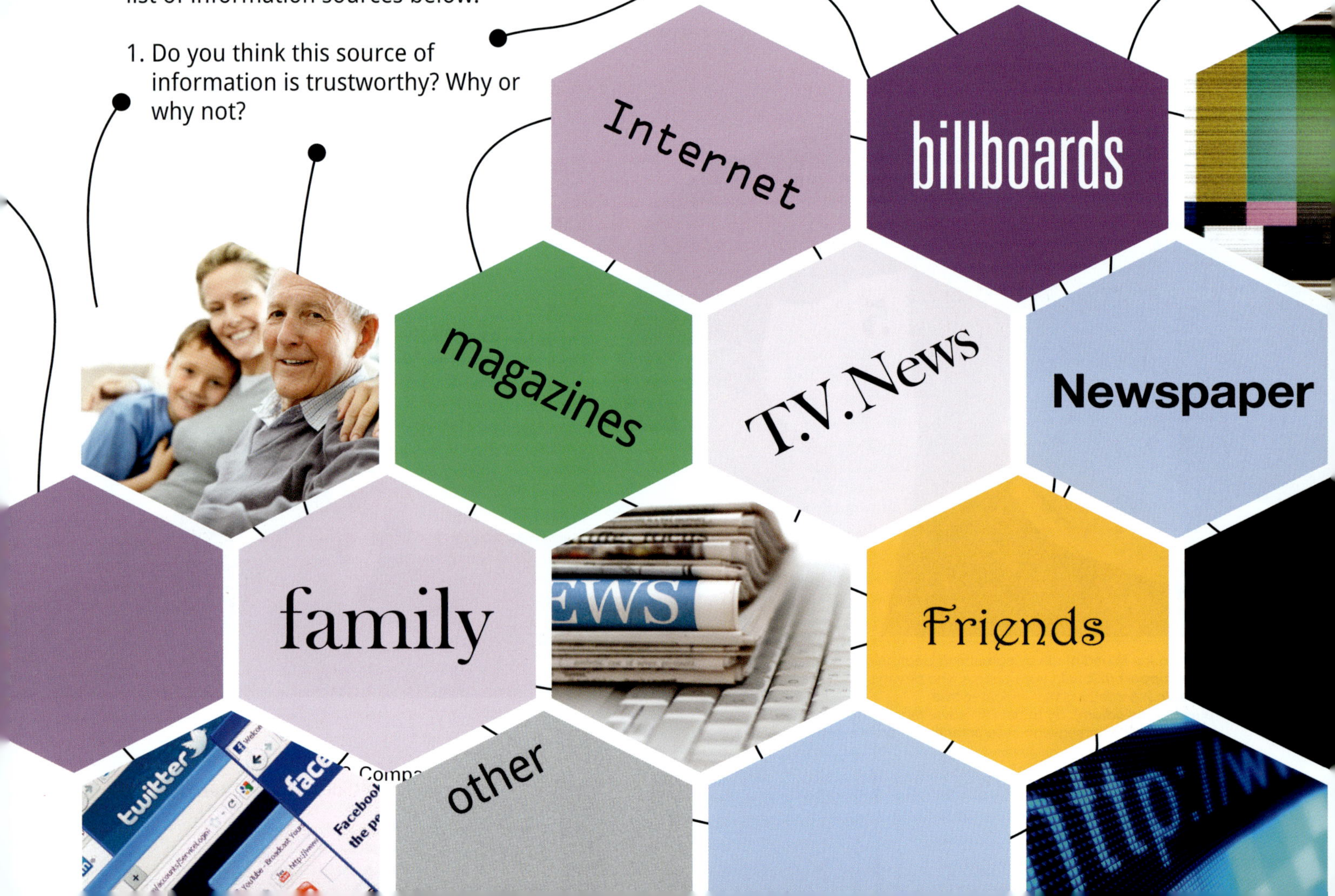

- Internet
- billboards
- magazines
- T.V. News
- Newspaper
- family
- Friends
- other

Now look at the picture below. Before listening to the conversation, make predictions about what you think is happening in this situation.

Listening TRACK 4-5

Now listen to the following dialogue, and see if your predictions were correct. Listen again and pay attention to the indirect questions.

Post-listening

Discuss what happened in the story. What is the problem? Have you ever experienced a situation where someone tried to **scam** you? Do you know someone who was scammed?

Do you think older people are more likely than young people to believe news sources or are they more **skeptical**? Why?

---

scam *(n.)*: to trick someone to give money
skeptical *(adj.)*: having doubts about something

Unit 2 Talk is Cheap | 31

C. Have You Heard...?

Act out the following situations. Change the direct questions to indirect questions and follow up by making some of your own questions. Use the chart on pg. 28 for help.

Example: Jim's weekend plans

1. What is Jim doing this weekend?
   A: *Do you know what Jim is doing this weekend?*
   B: *I'm not sure. He said something about maybe going to a party.*

2. Is he going scuba diving with his friends?
   A: *Did he say if he is going scuba diving with his friends?*
   B: *Ah, yes. He did say something about that...*

STUDENT A

1
Is there a new movie at the cinema?
(*Do you know...*)
- a. Where is it playing?
- b. What time is it playing?
- c. Is it interesting?

2
Is there an express train going to......?
(*Could you tell me...*)
- a. Where is the closest express train station?
- b. How often does it come?
- c. How long does it take?
- d. How much does it cost?

3
What English language courses are offered at this school?
- a. Do I have to take a level test?
- b. Are the courses good?
- c. How much are the course fees?

4
What kind of cell phone do you have?
- a. What company is it made by?
- b. What kind of features does it have?
- c. Do you like it?

STUDENT B

1
What area do you live in?
(*I was wondering...*)
- a. Is it a nice place?
- b. How long have you lived there?
- c. What is your house like?

2
Was Jack at the meeting yesterday?
(*Have you heard...*)
- a. Why didn't Jack come?
- b. Has he missed many meetings?
- c. Where is Jack now?

3
Do you have any cash?
- a. Could you lend me ten dollars?
- b. Can I borrow the money right now?
- c. When do I have to pay you back?

4
Did you see (*name of television show*) last night?
- a. What happened to the main character?
- b. What happened in the end?
- c. What do you think will happen next time?

3rd wheel
if you are the third member of this activity, offer different information than, or agree with, student B.

Discussion Questions

1 When do you have to start conversations with people you do not know?
   ▶ Do you remember a situation when you had to ask a stranger for help?

2 Who is the rudest person you have met?
   ▶ What was he or she like?

3 Do you find it difficult to interrupt other people?
   ▶ Why or why not?
   ▶ Do you dislike it when other people interrupt you?

4 Why do you think people like to listen to gossip?
   ▶ Have you heard any interesting gossip recently?

5 Do you feel comfortable asking friends for favors?
   ▶ What kinds of favors have you asked friends for?

6 Are you the kind of person who takes orders well, or do you hate being told what to do?
   ▶ Why do you think you are this way?

7 What would be some polite questions to ask the following people?
   ▶ Your professor
   ▶ Your parents
   ▶ The person sitting next to you on the subway
   ▶ A classmate
   ▶ A police officer

How about some impolite questions?

LESSON 2

>> WARM UP

Objectives:
/ Use tag questions

What is body language?

> Why is it important for communication?
> Have you ever had to communicate with someone who could not speak your language?
> What happened?

Part 1

Pretend that you are in another country and you do not speak the native language of that country. Act out the body language that you would use when you want to say the following:

- "Where's the bathroom?"
- "I'm lost! Where is the subway station?"
- "I want a small coffee to go."
- "Help! Someone just stole my wallet!"

Part 2

What are some other questions you might have to ask in a foreign country?
Make a list:

1 _____
2 _____
3 _____

Now decide how you would communicate these questions without being able to speak the language.

A. This Is Delicious, Isn't It?

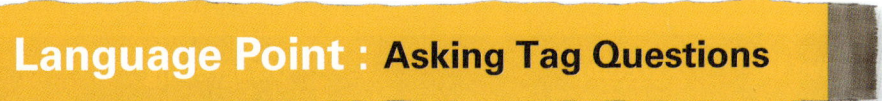
What's a tag? A tag is something small connected to something bigger, like a shirt tag.

Language Point: Asking Tag Questions

Speakers ask yes/no questions when they do not have previous knowledge about the topic.

Example: *Are you a vegetarian?*

Speakers generally ask tag questions when they have previous knowledge or expectations, but they want to check information or seek agreement.

Example: *You're a vegetarian, **aren't you?***
statement — question tag

Tip Informally it is common to replace the tag with the word: right.
You understand, right?

Statement
(+) Positive statement
The sky is blue,

(−) Negative statement
You don't like onions,

Questions tag
(−) Negative tag
isn't it?

(+) Positive tag
do you?

Part 1 ●

Complete each of the following questions by adding the appropriate tag.

1. You're a famous movie star, _____?
2. You have a coat, _____?
3. She's not from Canada, _____?
4. He should send his resume, _____?

Try these. They're a little bit harder.

5. He used to live in Sydney, _____?
6. Everyone came on time, _____?
7. Nobody has been to China, _____?

Unit 2 Talk is Cheap | 35

Language Point: Responding to Tag Questions

Positive statement + negative tag	Agreeing	Disagreeing
You *like* pizza, *don't* you?	Yes, I do.	No, I don't.
He *can* drive a car, *can't* he?	Yes, he can.	No, he can't.
They *are* alright, *aren't* they?	Yes, they are	No, they aren't.

Negative statement + positive tag	Agreeing	Disagreeing
It *isn't* cold outside, *is* it?	No, it isn't.	Yes, it is.
You *aren't* sick, *are* you?	No, I'm not.	Yes, I am.
He *isn't* married, *is* he?	No, he isn't.	Yes, he is.

◇ Note:
We sometimes add "actually" before the disagreeing statement. Actually, it is cold.

Part 2

Finish the tag question then match it to the appropriate response on the right.

1. This is good coffee, _____?   a. No, he doesn't.
2. You speak English, _____?   b. No, she wasn't.
3. You can come to my party, _____?   c. Yes, it is.
4. He doesn't like to study, _____?   d. No, I can't.
5. You will help me, _____?   e. Yes, I do.
6. She was absent yesterday, _____?   f. No, I won't.

B. You Don't, Do You?

Ask and respond to tag questions by doing the following:

1 One person asks the person on his/her left a tag question, using a positive or negative tag.
2 The second person should agree or disagree with the statement and give a reason why.
3 Repeat Steps 1-2 until all of the questions have been asked.

Example:

can drive
not be late
can't swim
can dance

A: *You can drive, can't you?*
B: *Yes I can. I have a driver's license. You won't be late, will you?*
C: *No, I won't. I'm always early. You can't swim, can you?*
D: *Actually, Yes I can. I learned when I was in elementary school. You can dance well, can't you?*

---

shouldn't smoke

haven't heard

will get embarrassed

often lie

can't sing well

ate too much again last night

don't like ice cream

won't get lost

---

have never worn makeup

enjoy gambling

don't study hard

don't like teachers

don't shower often

think Paris is beautiful

don't think English is boring

English is really hard

---

often skip class

are very beautiful

get angry sometimes

didn't sleep well

eat a lot of junk food

can't understand

believe Monday is better than Friday

shouldn't have done that

C. Tag Communication Party

Part 1 ● You are at a party with some of the Thompson's friends. Even though the guests are strangers, you have heard a little bit about each of them. Take on the roles of the various people at the party. Use tag questions to confirm or clarify information you have heard about the other people. For each question, role-play a follow-up discussion about that topic.

> **Example: Walter, Candy, and Todd**
>
> **Walter:** *So, Candy, you're a school teacher, aren't you?*
>
> **Candy:** *Yes, I am! I teach third grade Math.*
>
> **Walter:** *Do you like it?*
>
> **Candy:** *I love it. It is fun to teach children new things. Todd, you're a dance instructor, aren't you?*
>
> **Todd:** *Yes, I am!*

Part 2 ● Now make up your own character. Show your character's information to someone else and act out the situation again.

1. Your hobby _____

2. Your hometown _____

3. Something interesting about you _____

Discussion Questions

1. Are you good at **networking**?
   ▶ Do you use social network sites? Which ones?

2. Which sources of information are more **trustworthy** and accurate than others?
   ▶ Why do you think so?

3. How would life be different without the Internet and mobile phones?
   ▶ How would you communicate with your friends and family?

4. Do you prefer face-to-face communication, or do you prefer communicating through technology (e.g. Internet, mobile phone)?
   ▶ What advantages does each have?

5. When was the last time you had a **misunderstanding** with someone?
   ▶ Where were you?
   ▶ What happened?

6. How would you stay in touch with friends and family if you moved to another country?
   ▶ What problem does this kind of communication cause?

7. Is it important to learn about the culture of another country before traveling to that country?
   ▶ Why do you think so?

UNIT 2 REVIEW

How well can you use :
- ☐ Asking and responding to indirect questions?
- ☐ Asking and responding to tag questions?

What do you need to study more?

---

networking *(n.)*: getting to know other people for business purposes
misunderstanding *(n.)*: a mistake made while communicating
trustworthy *(adj.)*: something or someone that can be believed

Activity: 20 Questions

Work as a class or in small groups. One student chooses any person, place, or thing he or she can think of (Superman, the Pyramids, ice cream, etc.). The other students take turns asking questions to find out what person, place, or thing was chosen.

The questions should be of the "yes" or "no" variety. The person who chose can only respond with either "yes" or "no".

Start off with broad questions and then slowly narrow them down. You can only ask up to twenty questions.

Example:
Student A: *Is it something you eat?*
Student B: *Yes, it is.*
Student C: *Is it cold?*
Student B: *Yes.*
Student D: *It's ice cream, isn't it?*

Segue

Read the three following emails from Grandma Martha's inbox and decide which look legitimate and which look like scams:

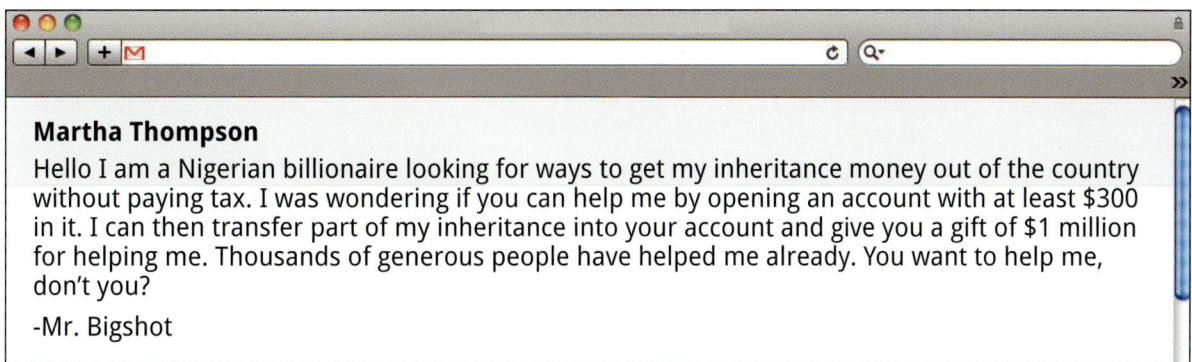

Martha Thompson

Hello I am a Nigerian billionaire looking for ways to get my inheritance money out of the country without paying tax. I was wondering if you can help me by opening an account with at least $300 in it. I can then transfer part of my inheritance into your account and give you a gift of $1 million for helping me. Thousands of generous people have helped me already. You want to help me, don't you?

-Mr. Bigshot

Mr. or Mrs. Martha Thompson

The internet is not always a safe and secure place! It is full of viruses and malware that can infect your computer. Your infected computer can be used by criminals to spam others, gain access to sensitive information, or even take over the world! By clicking on the link below you can download free software that will protect your computer.

http//:www.phishhook.com

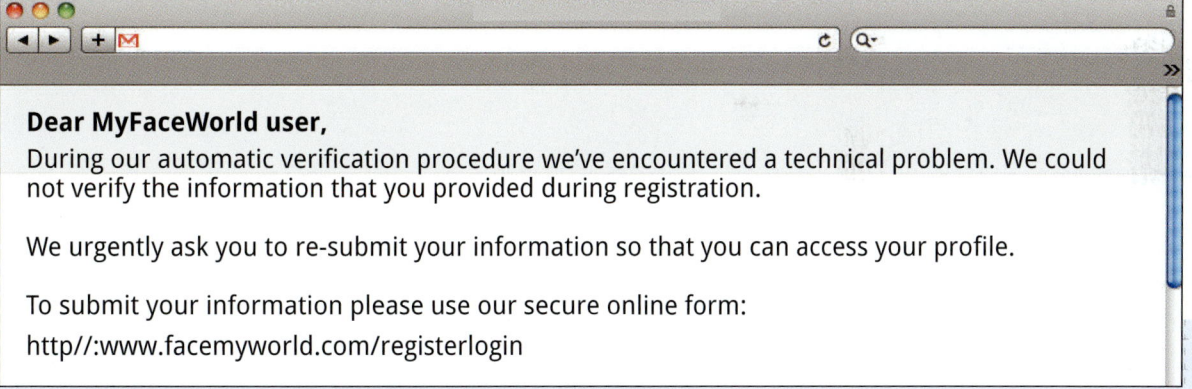

Dear MyFaceWorld user,

During our automatic verification procedure we've encountered a technical problem. We could not verify the information that you provided during registration.

We urgently ask you to re-submit your information so that you can access your profile.

To submit your information please use our secure online form:

http//:www.facemyworld.com/registerlogin

A. Discussion

1. Which emails look like **scams**? Why do you think so? Is the language used formal or informal?
2. Have you ever received scam emails? What did they promise or ask for?
3. Do you know any stories about people who were scammed by email or over the phone? What happened to them?
4. Do you think governments are doing enough to fight cybercrime? Is it possible to be safe on the Internet? What can we do to protect ourselves?

B. Writing

Write your own email scam of 6-8 sentences to Grandma. Try to make the scam as believable as possible.

Your teacher can decide who he/she thinks has written the best one.

03
There and Back Again
Travel and Transportation

Objectives:
/ Make decisions and choices about travel
/ Listen to a discussion about a trip

WARM UP

A. Discuss how you get to the following places. Be sure to be as specific as possible and ask follow-up questions.

How do you get to…

…your house from this class?

…your office or university from home?

…the nearest city from this city?

B. List as many forms of transportation as you can think of in the world. Which do you prefer? Why?

IDIOMS

- **in the same boat**
  We're both stuck in traffic and late for work. It looks like we're *in the same boat*.
- **hit the road**
  It's getting really late; I'd better *hit the road*.

COLLOCATIONS

- **take a holiday**
  We're *taking a holiday* to Spain.
- **go on a vacation**
  We're *going on a vacation* to Spain.

What Is It?

Explain the meaning with your partner.
- a guided tour
- to go sightseeing
- to book a ticket
- a layover

Unit 3 There and Back Again | 43

LESSON 1

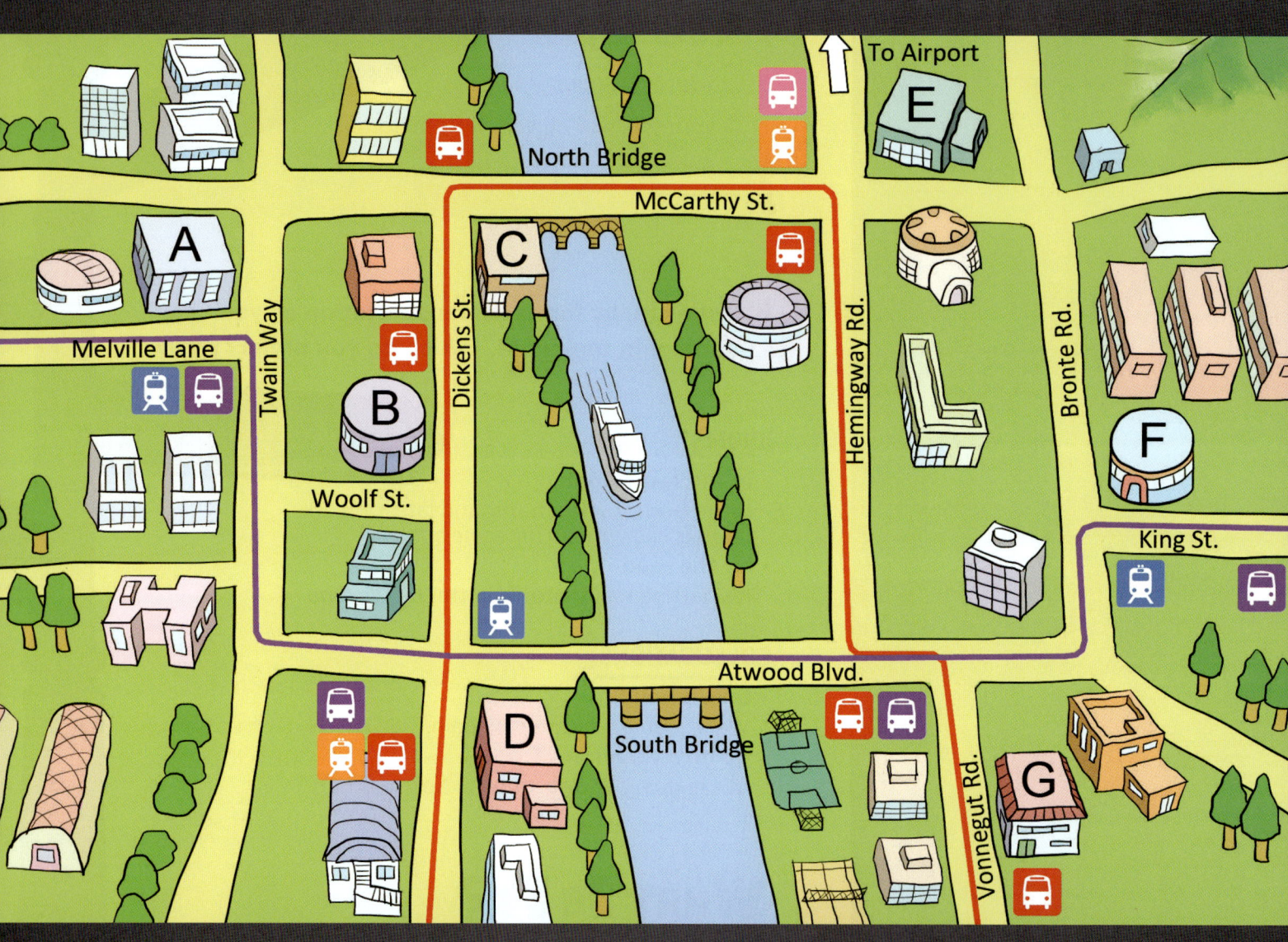

- **A** TechnoElectronic World
- **B** Special Kitty Day Care
- **C** The Daily Coffee Shop
- **D** Chapter 11 Bookstore
- **E** Fresh Family Grocery
- **F** Wok World Chinese Restaurant
- **G** The Thompson Home

Subway Station
= Blue Line and Orange Line

Airport Shuttle = Pink Bus

Bus Stops and Route
= Red Bus and Purple Bus

Did You Know?
"Get in" vs. "Get on"

These two phrasal verbs are very similar! When talking about travel, "get on" is generally used for vehicles in which you can stand, and "get in" is used for vehicles in which you must sit.

44 | SLE Generations 2 Compact

A. In a Rush

Answer the following questions by giving the most appropriate directions from the map.

1 In a car, what is the best way to get from Special Kitty Day Care to Wok World Chinese Restaurant?

2 What is the best way to get from TechnoElectronic World to Fresh Family Grocery using only public transportation?

3 Sally needs to get from Techno Electronic World to Chapter 11 Bookstore. She has lost her wallet, so she will have to walk.

• What is the fastest way for Sally to get to the bookstore?

4 Biff is driving Lisa home after their date, but he wants to spend as much time with her as he can.

• What is the slowest route Biff can take from the Daily Coffee Shop to the family home?

Need to Know:

- **to take a (taxi), to take a (left/right)**

  Why don't you **take a taxi** instead of the subway?

  When you get to Main Street, **take a left** on Melrose.

- **to get on a (bus/plane)**

  We **got on the bus** just outside the Museum of Modern Art.

- **to change (buses)**

  You will need **to change buses** at the library.

- **to transfer (subway lines)**

  When you get to City Station, you will need to **transfer** to Line 7.

5 Frick and Frack are distributing flyers to all of the local businesses.

• How can they go to each business without having to **backtrack**?

6 The Thompsons are running late to the airport. It's the middle of **rush hour** and there is a major traffic jam on both Hemingway Rd. and Bronte Rd.

• What is the quickest route?

7 Jack arrives home after class, and he finds a list of things his mother wants him to pick up before dinner. He needs to get a book his father ordered from the bookstore, and some cat food for Mr. Squiggles. The North Bridge is closed for the afternoon.

• What is the best way for Jack to take?

---

backtrack (v.): to return the same way you came
rush hour (n.): the busiest time for traffic before and after work

B. Bears, Bears, Bears

Pre-listening

1. Do you prefer relaxing and restful vacations, or vacations full of action and excitement?
   • What was the last restful or exciting vacation you took?

Now look at the picture below. Make predictions about what you think is happening in this situation.

2. Who wants to go where?
   • Do they all agree?
   • What kind of vacation is each of them hoping for?

Listening TRACK 6-7

After listening, look back at Question 2 and discuss how close your predictions were to the dialogue.

Post-listening

Mark the following statements based on the listening with True (T), False (F), or if there is not enough information, a question mark (?). If the answer is False, make it into a true statement.

1	T ☐ F ☐ ? ☐	The family is planning their winter vacation.
2	T ☐ F ☐ ? ☐	Richard and Susan want to go on a cruise.
3	T ☐ F ☐ ? ☐	Lisa thinks there is a lot to do on a cruise ship.
4	T ☐ F ☐ ? ☐	The cruise offers chances to gamble, golf, and see theatre.
5	T ☐ F ☐ ? ☐	Susan likes her daughter's idea of going skydiving.
6	T ☐ F ☐ ? ☐	Jack wants to go camping in the mountains.
7	T ☐ F ☐ ? ☐	Richard took Jack and Lisa camping last year.
8	T ☐ F ☐ ? ☐	The cruise ship is full of bears.

C. When in Rome...or is that Egypt?

- Making recommendations and suggestions
- Giving advice
- Comparisons

Part 1

Rank the following items in order of importance (1=Most important, 6=Least important) when choosing a summer vacation destination:

- **Food**
- **Temperature**
- **Shopping**
- **Popular tourist attractions**
- **Cost**
- **Distance from home**

Compare your ranking with a partner, and ask follow-up questions.

> **Example:**
>
> **A:** *I think tourist attractions are the most important part of a vacation.*
>
> **B:** *Oh, I think food is the most important part. Why do you think the number of tourist attractions is so important?*
>
> **A:** *I really love to take pictures when I go on vacation.*

Part 2

You want to go on summer vacation together for a week, but you do not know where to go. Your budget for the week is $900. Look at the country profiles below and choose <u>one</u> destination. Make sure to <u>compare</u> your options and ask follow-up questions.

> **Example:**
>
> **A:** *We need to take a vacation! Where do you think we should go?*
>
> **B:** *Well, what types of activities do you enjoy in the summer?*
>
> **A:** *I really like to take walks and go surfing.*
>
> **B:** *Okay. Maybe we could go to Costa Rica or Iceland.*
>
> **A:** *Hmmm...the temperature in Iceland might be cold. How about Kenya? The hotel cost is cheaper than the hotel in Costa Rica.*

Cairo, Egypt

Hotel Cost: $250 for the week
Temperature: 45°C
Activities: (for one person)
- Go to the Cairo International Film Festival, $40
- Go on a Pyramid tour, $20
- Go on a Nile River dinner cruise, $30

Food: $15 for one meal

Tokyo, Japan

Hotel Cost: $490 for the week
Temperature: 33°C
Activities: (for one person)
- Visit Tokyo Disney, $60
- Go to a Japanese garden, $8
- Visit Tokyo Sky Tree, $10

Food: $30 for one meal

Edinburgh, Scotland

Hotel Cost: $400 for the week
Temperature: 20°C
Activities: (for one person)
- Visit Edinburgh Castle, $20
- Watch a performance at Edinburgh Festival Theatre, $15
- Go shopping on Princes Street, $100

Food: $20 for one meal

Nairobi, Kenya

Hotel Cost: $150 for the week
Temperature: 40°C
Activities: (for one person)
- Visit Langata Giraffe Centre, $20
- Go shopping at the Village Market, $50
- Visit traditional tribal villages, $15

Food: $5 for one meal

San Jose, Costa Rica

Hotel Cost: $200 for the week

Temperature: 27°C

Activities: (for one person)
- Go on a rainforest tour, $20
- Take surfing lessons, $15
- Go horseback riding, $20
- Go river rafting, $15

Food: $10 for one meal

Reykjavík, Iceland

Hotel Cost: $300 for the week

Temperature: 18°C

Activities: (for one person)
- Go whale watching, $200
- Viking museum, $10
- Go hiking, free
- Going to the beach, free
- Enjoying hot springs, $15

Food: $25 for one meal

Athens, Greece

Hotel Cost: $200 for the week

Temperature: 40°C

Activities: (for one person)
- Visit Greek temples, $15
- Go to the Athens Municipal Art Gallery, $25
- Visit site of the first Olympic games, $10

Food: $15 for one meal

Atlanta, Georgia

Hotel Cost: $300 for the week

Temperature: 32°C

Activities: (for one person)
- Visit Coca-Cola headquarters, $10
- Visit Georgia Aquarium (world's largest indoor aquarium), $20
- Watch a performance at Centennial Olympic Park, $15

Food: $15 for one meal

Discussion Questions

1. What is your preferred type of public transportation?
   - Which form of public transportation is your least favorite?

2. What was the most recent trip you took?
   - How did you get there and what kinds of transportation did you use?
   - How long did the trip take?
   - What about the cost, weather, and activities?

3. What are the advantages and disadvantages of owning your own car?

4. Where would you most like to travel to?
   - Why would you like to go there?

5. Have you ever traveled to another city or country that you prefer over your own?
   - Would you prefer to live in that place?
   - If not, why do you think your city or country is the best place to live?

6. How do you think travel and transportation will change in the next 20 years?

7. When foreign friends visit your country, what do you suggest that they see and do?
   - Why would you recommend these sights and activities?
   - How would you suggest they get around?

LESSON 2

>> WARM UP
Look at the following traffic signs and discuss what you think the meaning is for each.

Objectives:
/ Talk about likely and unlikely situations with conditionals

A. What Will Happen If...

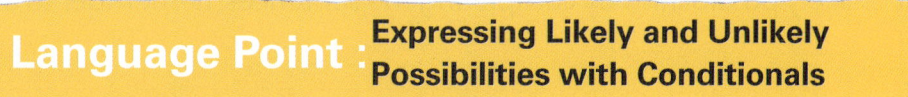
Language Point: Expressing Likely and Unlikely Possibilities with Conditionals

To express likely possibilities:

> if + present tense, will + verb

Example
- *If it rains, I will get wet.*
- *I will be able to buy my dream car if I get this job.*

To express unlikely events or unreal circumstances:

> if + simple past tense, would/could + verb

Example
- *If you won the lottery, you could go on a cruise to the Bahamas.*
- *I would fly to Paris, if I were a bird.*

◇ Note: 'were' is used for both singular and plural subjects.

Match the following sentence halves to make complete sentences. Say whether you agree or disagree with the statements.

Real Situations

1 If I lose my wallet ...	a ... he will not be able to leave the country.
2 You will get lost in Seoul ...	b ... if you **book the tickets** in advance.
3 You will arrive at your destination faster...	c ... if you take the express train.
4 If a tourist loses his passport...	d ... if you do not speak Korean.
5 Airfare will be cheaper...	e ... I will have to call the credit card company.

Unreal Situations

1 If you went to Paris...	a ...we would have to walk home.
2 If we got into a car accident...	b ...I would not have any clothes to wear.
3 If the airline lost my luggage...	c ...you could go swimming.
4 You could get a sunburn ...	d ...you would need to speak a little French.
5 If you had brought your swim suit...	e ...if you weren't wearing **sunscreen**.

book *(v.)*: to reserve a space
sunscreen *(n.)*: lotion put on the skin to prevent sunburn

B. If I Had My Way

Practice talking about unlikely possibilities by completing the sentences. Remember to ask follow-up questions.

> **Example:**
> **A:** *If I were rich, I would buy an apartment in London.*
> **B:** *Where in London would you want to live?*

If I got a new pet…

…if I studied English every day.

…if it snowed next week.

If I were given plane tickets to go anywhere…

If our teacher quit his/her job in the middle of class…

If I had my favorite celebrity over for dinner…

If I could change one thing about myself…

…if a large meteor from space were going to destroy the planet in ten days.

C. A Three-Hour Tour

Part 1 ● The Thompson family is out to sea and suddenly the yacht they are sailing on begins to sink! They only have time to take five items from the ship and safely get to a nearby island. Decide which items they should take with them. Remember, they could be on the island for many weeks or months!

> **Example:** If they **take** the volleyball, they **won't** get bored.

Part 2 ● On This Island

You're stranded on the island with the Thompson Family! What would you do in the following situations? The only items you have available are what you chose in Part 1 and things you might find on a desert island.

1. You need a place to rest but the ground on the island is very rocky and uncomfortable. *I would…….*

2. It's the middle of the night. You hear a strange sound in the woods.

3. You find the source of the sound – it's a large wild pig. He runs at you!

4. You are getting hungry on the island. You find a banana tree, but there is a **raging** river between you and it.

5. You find a few chickens, but if you decide to kill them and eat them raw, you might get very sick.

6. You meet a tribe of **cannibals** who don't understand your language. They look hungry.

7. One night, a very big storm comes. It starts **raining cats and dogs**.

8. You see a ship on the **horizon**. If you get their attention, you can go home!

raging *(adj.)*: very strong force
cannibal *(n)*: an animal that eats its own kind
raining cats and dogs *(idiom)*: raining very hard
horizon *(n.)*: the line where the earth meets the sky

Discussion Questions

1 If you were an animal, what would you be?

2 If you could only wear one piece of clothing, what would it be?

3 If you had a time machine, when and where would you go?

4 What would you do if you found a wallet on the street? Why?

5 If you had to lose one of your five senses, which one would you lose?

6 If you could only eat one type of meal for the rest of your life, what would it be?

7 If you had the power to change three things about the world, what would you change?

8 What would you do if you could be **invisible** for one day?

9 If you could choose to have a son or daughter, which would you choose and why?

UNIT 3 REVIEW

How well can you use:
- [ ] travel and transportation vocabulary?
- [ ] expressing likely and unlikely possibilities?
- [ ] decision making skills?

What do you need to study more?

invisible *(adj)*: unable to be seen

Activity: Riddle-de-dum

The Problem:

A man has to get a fox, a chicken, and a sack of corn across a river. He has a rowboat, but it can only carry him and one other thing.
If the fox and the chicken are left together, the fox will eat the chicken.
If the chicken and the corn are left together, the chicken will eat the corn.
How does the man do it?

HINT !

Some items might have to cross the river more than once.

While solving the riddle
Ask your partners:
- What would happen if the man took the _____ first?
- What would happen if the man took the _____ next?

58 | SLE Generations 2 Compact

Family Rescued on Desert Island

By **Lawson D. Woods**, PNN

In a dramatic story of survival, the Thompson family was rescued from a previously unknown island yesterday. The Thompsons got on a small tour boat during their vacation which sank an hour later. The family was mostly unhurt, well fed, and appeared happy.

The family managed to survive their six-week ordeal with only five items they salvaged from the sinking ship. "Lisa suggested if we brought the sleeping bags we would be comfortable." said Jack Thompson.

It wasn't just a bad night's sleep the Thompsons had to deal with. "Dad recommended that if we brought the gun we could protect ourselves. A good idea because a wild pig attacked our camp." said Lisa Thompson, "And Mom brought the rope. Because she brought the rope, we could cross that river for the bananas!"

The Thompsons, however, were not alone. The island was also populated by cannibals. "It was Lisa that saved us," said Susan Thompson, "She claimed if we brought the novel we could read aloud. It turns out the cannibals love having Harry Potter read to them even though they can't understand our language. Who knew?" The Thompsons plan on returning home to their cat, Mr. Squiggles, and never going on a cruise again.

A. Discussion
1. What items did the family bring with them?
   Why did they bring each one?
   Were these the same items you chose to bring?
2. Do you think it would be possible for you to survive out in the wilderness for several weeks or more?
    Why do you think so?
3. If you could choose to go somewhere and be alone for a month, where would you go?

B. Writing
Write a short paragraph telling the story from another character's perspective. For example, one of the tour boat operators, the rescuers, or even one of the cannibals.

WARM UP

What chores have you done recently?
Who does these things in your house?

- do the dishes
- fold the laundry
- take the trash out
- pay the bills
- cook dinner
- clean the bathroom

What are some things other people have done for you recently?

PHRASAL VERBS

- **get up**
- **sleep in**
  I have to *get up* every day at six, so this weekend I'm *sleeping in*.
- **clean up**
  We had a big party last night and the house needs to be *cleaned up*.

COLLOCATIONS

- **check my teeth/eyes/health**
- **run erra nds**
  I have to *run* a lot of *errands* today and get my *eyes checked*.

IDIOMS

- **at the crack of dawn**
  My uncle goes to work at the *crack of dawn*.
- **run like clockwork**
  I have to get my car serviced every three months, but after that it *runs like clockwork*.

Unit 4 A Day in the Life | 61

LESSON 1

A. Who Kicked Mr. Squiggles?

Language Point : Passive Voice

Active Voice
Active sentences say the subject does something to the object.
Who kicked Mr. Squiggles?

Bill is the focus of the sentence, and the one doing the action.

subject	**verb**	**object**
Bill	kicked	Mr. Squiggles.

Passive Voice
What if we do not know who performed the action? Mr. Squiggles becomes the subject. Who performed the action is not important.
What happened to Mr. Squiggles?

subject	**to be + past participle**	**object**
Mr. Squiggles	was kicked.	(unknown)

A passive sentence can also include the phrase **(by+someone)**. This is to make it understood that it was Bill who performed the action and not Ted.
Was Mr. Squiggles kicked by Bill or Ted?

subject	**to be + past participle**	**by + object**
Mr. Squiggles	was kicked	by Bill.

◇ Note: Only verbs that are transitive (verbs that can take an object) can be used in the passive. Intransitive verbs cannot be used in passive sentences.

Example: *I slept for eight hours last night. I got up at ten o'clock.*

Part 1 Change these forms into passive questions. Ask and answer the questions. Ask follow-up questions.

> **Who/service/your family car**
> **A:** *Who is your car serviced by?*
> **B:** *My car is serviced by Fonzi's garage.*
> **A:** *How often do you take your car there for service?*

1. Who / make / the best coffee
2. Where / sell / good quality clothes
3. Who / write / your favorite book
4. Who / make / the best pizza
5. When / celebrate / your favorite holiday
6. Who / make / your shoes
7. Who / cut / your hair
8. Who / check / your teeth

Part 2 Describe Mr. Squiggles' typical day using both the active and passive voice.

> **A:** *Jack **plays** with Mr. Squiggles in the morning. What happens after that?*
> **B:** *Mr. Squiggles **feels exhausted** by the fun.*

Mr. Squiggles' typical day

B. The Case of the Consumed Cream Cake

Susan spent two days making a very special cake. On Monday night at 7 p.m., she left the house to run a few **errands**. When she returned at 8 p.m., half of the cake had been eaten! She called a meeting of everyone in the house, but nobody admitted responsibility.

Listening TRACK 8-9

As you listen, fill in the chart to find out who might have committed the crime.

errand *(n.)*: small job to collect or deliver something
narrow down *(phrasal v.)*: to limit the amount of things being considered

	Richard (Husband)	Lisa (Daughter)	Jack (Son)	Martha and Charles (In-laws)	Mr. Squiggles (Cat)
At home during the time of the crime					
Doesn't like strawberry					
Has brown hair					
Found with icing on them					

Post-listening

Now that you've **narrowed down** the suspects, here are a few more clues:

Scratches on the table

Unopened snacks on the table

Cat food cans laying on the floor

Looking at the new clues and the information you collected from the chart above, discuss:
- who you think is the most likely suspect?
- why you think they did it?

Unit 4 A Day in the Life | 65

C. I Said Hey, What's Going On?

- Past progressive
- Because and Since

Look at the picture and start with what happened. Then, use the verbs below to explain how the story happened in reverse. Try to use as many verbs as you can in each story.

Example:
A: *The dog's leg was broken by a scooter.* **Why?**
B: *Because he was chasing Mr. Squiggles down the street.* **Why?**
C: *Since his food was stolen by Mr. Squiggles.* **Why?**

spill
throw out
fall
cut
knock over
catch
ruin
slap
smash

Discussion Questions

1 What kinds of things do you do every day?
- ▶ How about once a month?

2 What time have you been getting up and going to bed recently?
- ▶ What do you think the advantages and disadvantages of being a morning or a night person are?

3 What do you usually have for breakfast?
- ▶ Who makes your breakfast every morning?

4 Who does the following chores in your house: (answer with passive voice)
- ▶ do the dishes
- ▶ fold the laundry
- ▶ take the trash out
- ▶ mop the floor
- ▶ cook dinner
- ▶ clean the bathroom

5 Are you pretty good at **sticking to a schedule**, or do you usually **run late**?
- ▶ Why?

6 What personal activities (hobbies, sports, interests) do you make a part of your daily routine?
- ▶ How do you feel when you don't have time for them?

7 Do you usually wake up at the **crack of dawn**, or do you **sleep in**?
- ▶ Why? What are the advantages and disadvantages of each?

sticking to a schedule *(idiom):* following a routine closely
run late *(idiom):* not coming at a scheduled time
crack of dawn *(idiom):* very early in the morning
sleep in *(phrasal v.):* sleep until late in the day

LESSON 2

>> WARM UP

Objectives:
/ Use causative passive
/ Review giving advice
/ Review likely and unlikely possibilities

Look at the pictures below and discuss the following questions:
> What things are done by these people at work?
> What skills do these people need for work?

water, arrange

cut, wash

serve, make

change, service

prepare, cook

68 | SLE Generations 2

A. Hotel Management

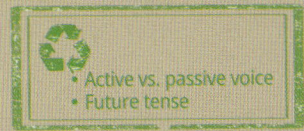

You are general managers in a hotel. The schedules for this week are incomplete. Ask questions using the active voice, and answer questions with the passive voice to complete the schedules. Use the verbs next to the department name to help you.

Example:

A: *Who will manage the front desk on Sunday?*

B: *The front desk **will be managed** by Matt on Sunday.*

A: *Who is going to cook the food on Wednesday?*

B: *The food **is going to be cooked** by Chef Jeremy on Wednesday.*

STUDENT A

Department	Area	Sun.	Mon.	Tues.	Wed.	Thurs.	Fri.	Sat.
Front Desk	front desk (manage)	Matt		Lisa		Matt	Lisa	Matt
Housekeeping	rooms (clean)		Annette	Emilio	Carl	Annette		Emilio
Restaurant	restaurant (supervise)	Rod		Rod	Sarah		Sarah	Sarah
Bar	bar (staff)	Brian	Joseph	Hillary		Joseph	Hillary	
Kitchen	food (cook)	Chef Todd	Chef Jaime		Chef Jeremy		Chef Jeremy	Chef Rudy
Banquets	banquets (organize)	Jeff	Gary		David	Gary		Tony
Sales	rooms (sell)		Heather	Carolyn	Cheryl	Carolyn	Heather	

Unit 4 A Day in the Life | 69

STUDENT B

Department	Area	Sun.	Mon.	Tues.	Wed.	Thurs.	Fri.	Sat.
Front Desk	front desk (manage)	Matt	Valerie		Shirley		Lisa	Matt
Housekeeping	rooms (clean)	Annette		Emilio	Carl	Annette	Carl	
Restaurant	restaurant (supervise)		Brandon	Rod	Sarah	Rod		Sarah
Bar	bar (staff)	Brian	Joseph		Mason		Hillary	Hillary
Kitchen	food (cook)	Chef Todd	Chef Jaime	Chef Todd		Chef Rudy	Chef Jeremy	
Banquets	banquets (organize)			Tony	David	Gary	Jeff	Tony
Sales	rooms (sell)	Cheryl	Heather	Carolyn		Carolyn		Heather

3rd wheel
Write down the schedule as you hear it, checking that the information is correct as you go.

B. What a Beautiful Day in the Neighborhood

Language Point : Causative Passive

We can use this form to say we are having something done for us.
The person who pays for or orders the action is the subject of the sentence. Use either the verb have or get, then a passive phrase as the object.

Subject	Verb	Object + Past Participle
I	get/have	my nails done by a manicurist.

PART 1 ● Change the sentences to show that you caused something to happen using the causative passive and a by phrase to say who performed the action.

1 **My car is serviced.**

2 **A pizza was delivered.**

3 **My suits are cleaned.**

4 **Our family portrait was taken.**

5 **My teeth are checked.**

6 **The dog was groomed.**

PART 2 ● When Susan and Richard first got married, they lived in a terrible neighborhood, but they fixed up their house and made it beautiful. Use the causative passive to describe what Richard or Susan had done and by whom. See if you can find at least 10 improvements.

Example:

A: *What did Richard and Susan do with the lawn?*
B: *They had the grass cut by Larry's Lawn Service.*

Possible verbs:

- Clean
- Fix
- Paint
- Pull
- Remove
- Replace
- Cut
- Install
- Plant
- Sweep
- Repair
- Water

People for hire:

- Larry's Lawn Service
- The Fence Doctor
- Handyman Harry
- Sunny Windows
- Part Time Painters
- A-1 Garage
- Green Gardeners
- Crime Busters CCTV
- Rascal Roofer

fix up*(phrasal v.)*: to repair or improve

C. Decisions, Decisions, Decisions…

Take turns asking for and giving advice for each of the following situations. Make sure to use the passive voice in your answers.

Example:

Getting a pet: fish, dog, alligator

A: *I'm thinking about **getting a pet** and need some advice. If you were me, would you get a fish, a dog, or an alligator?*

B: *I would get a fish. If you got a fish, you wouldn't need a big apartment. Also, fish **are fed** just once a day, so they are cheap. If you bought a dog, you would need more time and money because dogs **are fed** twice a day, and they have to be walked outside.*

STUDENT A

1 Getting a new job: police officer, tour guide, high school teacher

2 Being in a relationship: stay single forever, get married this year, get married 10 years from now

3 Going to work/school: bicycle, car, public transportation

4 Taking a vacation: going on an African safari, skiing in Canada, shopping in Paris

5 Breaking up with someone: over the phone, by letter, face to face

6 Going on a date: art museum, café, amusement park

7 Getting in shape: jogging, weight lifting, boxing

8 Eating dinner: cooking spaghetti, ordering pizza, going to a Chinese restaurant

Unit 4 A Day in the Life | 73

STUDENT B

3rd wheel
Give alternative advice, or agree with the person giving advice.

1. Studying for a test: alone, with four friends, at an institute

2. Making new friends: salsa lessons, English class, internet

3. Studying abroad: Philippines, Canada, England

4. Buying a home: small apartment in the city, house in the country, sailboat

5. Making plans for this weekend: gambling at a casino, playing computer games, watching a musical

6. Buying a computer: laptop, desktop, tablet

7. Having broken your friend's laptop: lie, tell the truth, buy her a new one

8. Winning $1,000: new clothes, weekend at a 5-star hotel, savings account

Example:

Getting a pet: cat, bird, snake

A: *I'm thinking about **getting a pet** and need some advice. If you were me, would you get a cat, a bird, or a snake?*

B: *I would get a snake because snakes **are fed** only once a month. If you get a bird, you will have to take care of it forever because birds live so long.*

Discussion Questions

1. Have you ever had clothes made for you?
   - ▶ What did you have made and for what occasion?
   - ▶ If not, what would you like to have made?
2. Where do you usually go to have your hair cut?
   - ▶ Why do you prefer that place to others?
3. When was the last time you had your photo taken professionally?
4. If you could have any one of the following services provided for you free of charge for a year, which would you choose and why?
   - ▶ **chauffeuring**
   - ▶ professional massage
   - ▶ cooking by a chef
   - ▶ house cleaning
   - ▶ hairstyling
   - ▶ personal fitness trainer
5. If you had a robot that could perform various household chores and run errands, what would you have it do?
6. Have you ever had your fortune told?
   - ▶ Do you believe in fortune tellers? Why or why not?
7. Have you ever **played a trick** on someone or had a trick played on you?
   - ▶ What happened?
8. How often do have your teeth checked?
   - ▶ How about your vision?
   - ▶ How about your health?

UNIT 4 REVIEW

How well can you use:
- ☐ Active voice vs. passive voice?
- ☐ Causative passive?

What do you need to study more?

chauffeuring *(n.)*: personal driving service
play a trick *(idiom)*: to trick someone into believing something as a joke

Activity

: The Case of the Disappearing Family Man

A man named Sam Smith suddenly disappeared. He seemed happily married with two children and a good job in a bank. Everyone is confused. Where is he? Did he leave on his own? If so, why? Was he kidnapped? Look over the clues below, and try to figure out what happened. When you are done, present your version of the events to the rest of your class. See who came up with the best explanation for Sam's disappearance.

The following clues were found:

- Part of a handwritten note saying, "...never want to see you again... don't try to get in touch with me. Jane..."
- A $100 bill
- A page torn out of a phone book containing information about travel agencies
- A photo of a young woman wearing a bikini
- A photo of the same woman sitting on an office desk
- Two symphony tickets for Wednesday evening at 8pm
- Another handwritten letter reading "...I know it's the coward's way out, but I really had no choice. You may not believe me, but I do still love you and only wish everything turned out..."
- A guidebook entitled, "Navigating the Seven Seas"
- A notice of resignation to take effect in two weeks
- An advertisement circled in red, reading "Yacht for Sale"
- A job advertisement for an accounts manager taken from a newspaper
- A company credit card with receipts for lunches, jewelry, hotel rooms, etc.

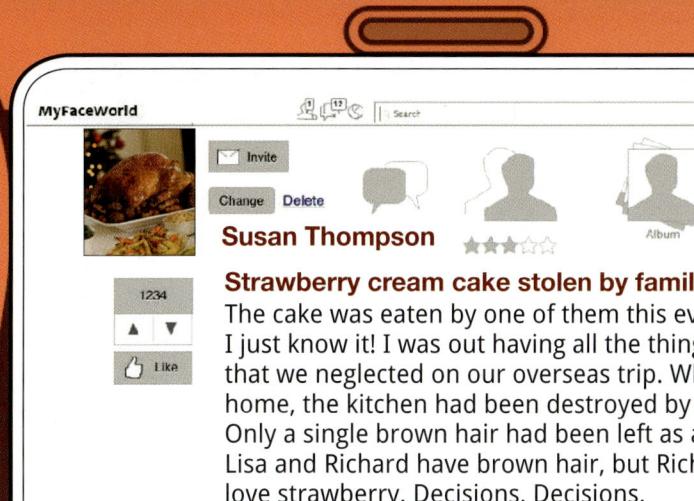

Segue

Susan Thompson

Strawberry cream cake stolen by family!
The cake was eaten by one of them this evening. I just know it! I was out having all the things done that we neglected on our overseas trip. When I came home, the kitchen had been destroyed by the thief. Only a single brown hair had been left as a clue. Both Lisa and Richard have brown hair, but Rich and Jack love strawberry. Decisions. Decisions.

Lisa T.
Oh Mom! Give it up. I told you that on my way home from the market I stopped to get my nails done. I was really hungry, but strawberry is so barf! I'm sure the cake was eaten by Jack. He's so lazy. The laundry wasn't done because he was probably stuffing his face.

The Jackster
Is your homework done, Sis? Ma, I didn't do it! Okay the laundry wasn't done, but I was distracted because the cat was already fed. He wasn't begging so we spent some time playing with a string. Besides, it was Dad who went to bed not feeling very well.

Rich Thompson
Hold on Jack. I was out having my hair cut and I bought a bag of chips on the way home, so I couldn't have been that hungry. The cake was eaten by someone with a large appetite. I'm looking at you, Lisa.

A. Discussion

1. Have you ever been in a situation with family or friends where you disagreed over what exactly happened?
   - What was the disagreement about?
   - How did you solve the problem?

2. What does each family member claim to have been doing during the time the crime took place?
   - Given this new information, do you think any of them are more suspicious than others?

B. Writing

As a friend, write a response to Susan of five to six sentences telling her who you think might have committed the crime and what their motives might have been.

WARM UP

Brainstorm as many different natural disasters as you can think of.

COLLOCATIONS

- **Take precautions**
  Please make sure to *take precautions*, like fastening your seatbelt, before you drive a car.

PHRASAL VERBS

- **Reach out**
  The disaster was terrible, but it gave us an opportunity to *reach out* and help one another.
- **Watch out**
  Be careful to *watch out* for pickpockets when visiting the city.

IDIOMS

- **Better to be safe than sorry**
- **An accident waiting to happen**
  Putting the cup on the edge of the window is just an *accident waiting to happen*. Put it on the floor. It's *better to be safe than sorry*.
- **Keep your cool**
  Don't panic! *Keep your cool,* and walk slowly away from the bear.

TONGUE TWISTER

The thirty-three thieves thought they thrilled the throne through Thursday.
There those thousand thinkers were thinking, where did those other three thieves go through.

Unit 5 Better Safe Than Sorry | 79

LESSON 1

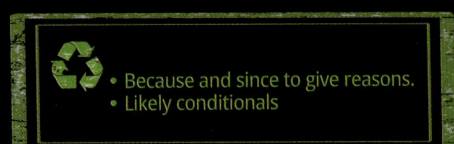
- Because and since to give reasons.
- Likely conditionals

A. What Do I Do?!

Discuss what solutions are possible for the personal emergencies below.

Example: Animal Attack - You are walking in the park when a dog attacks you.

A: *What would you do?*
B: *If a dog attacked me, I'd grab it and take it with me to the hospital.*
A: *Really? Why?*
B: *To make sure it doesn't have rabies.*

ACCIDENTS

1. **Car Crash** You are driving in the countryside when you come across a car that has hit a tree.
2. **Passport** You are traveling in a foreign country when you realize you've lost your passport.
3. **Phone** You get a new smart phone, but just a few hours later you drop it in a public toilet!

SOCIAL EMERGENCIES

1. **Food Poisoning** You are out with your boyfriend or girlfriend having dinner when suddenly you become very ill.
2. **Wardrobe Malfunction** You bend down to pick up a pencil at work and your pants rip up the middle.
3. **Mr. Squiggles!** Your cat has climbed up a very tall tree and is too scared to climb back down.

DISASTERS

1. **Gas Leak** You wake up in the night and smell a strong odor like rotten eggs coming from the kitchen.
2. **Grease Fire** Your friend is cooking something on the stove when suddenly the grease in the pan catches fire.
3. **Localized Flood** While driving to work, you try to cross an intersection that is full of water, and suddenly the car starts floating!

CRIME

1. **Burglary** You come home from a weekend trip. You notice that the front door of your house is open.
2. **Hit and Run** You see a child crossing the street when she's hit by a scooter. The scooter driver **takes off**.
3. **Identity Theft** You get a call from your bank asking why you bought ten new computers yesterday.

take off *(phrasal verb)*: to run away suddenly and quickly

Unit 5 Better Safe Than Sorry | 81

B. When It Rains, It Pours

It rained forty days and forty nights at the Thompson household. What was damp became a puddle. A puddle became a pool. A pool became a small lake.

Pre-listening

Imagine that you just found out that your entire house is going to flood within an hour. You can only take three things with you.
What would you choose?

_____
_____
_____

Listening TRACK 10-11

While listening, check the items Richard and Susan decide to pack before **evacuating** their house.

Guitar ☐	Computer ☐	Baby Blanket ☐	Photo Album ☐
Family Quilt ☐	Family Pet ☐	Jewelry Box ☐	Important Documents ☐
Trophy ☐	Television ☐	Medication ☐	Hard Drive ☐

evacuate (v.): to remove someone from a dangerous situation

Post-listening

1. Which items did the family decide to take?
   • Did they leave right away?

2. Which items did they leave or forget?
   • What do you think will happen to the items they left?

3. Does it ever flood in your city?
   • Do you know anyone who has been affected by a flood?

What precautions could you take to avoid or prepare for the following emergencies?

Choose from the list below and add your own recommendations.

- Earthquake
- Heart Attack
- Fire
- Flood
- Tsunami
- **Mugging**

- **Teach family members how to turn off gas, electricity, and water.**
- **Identify safe places in each room.**
- **Stick to well-lit and well-populated areas.**
- **Don't walk with your smart phone or wallet in your hand.**
- **Plan and practice an evacuation route.**
- **Keep important documents in a water-tight bag or safe.**
- **Lower the amount of greasy and salty food you eat.**
- **Exercise often and reduce stress.**
- **Install smoke detectors in every room.**

mug (v.): to rob someone on the street

C. Well, You Really Should...

Language Point : Strength of Advice or Commands

Mary thinks she is allergic to her lip gloss. What do you think she should do?

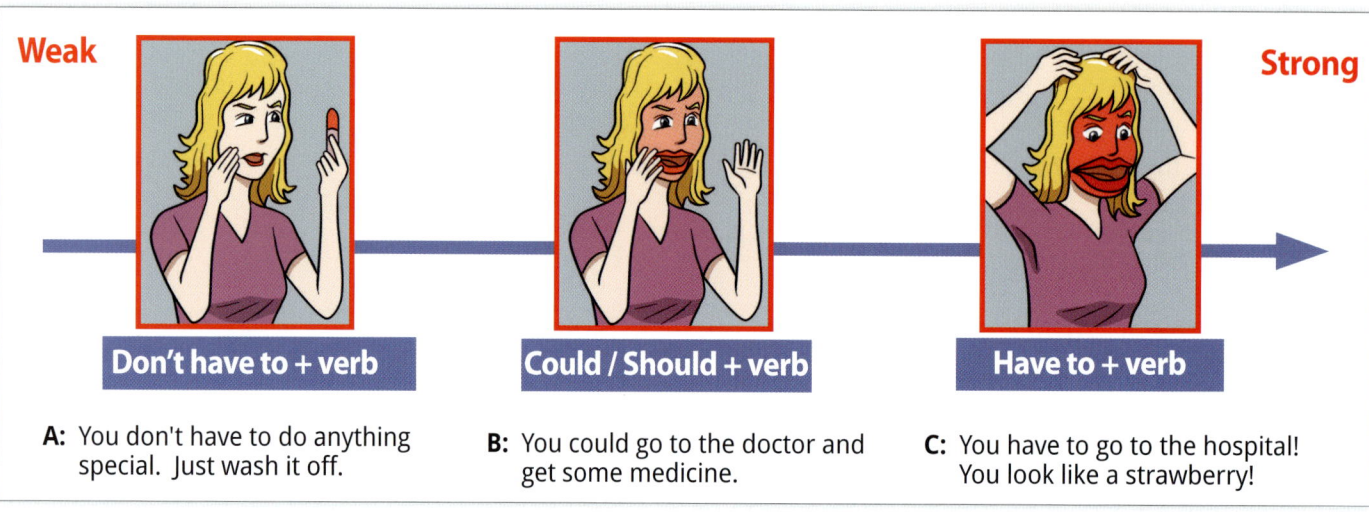

A: You don't have to do anything special. Just wash it off.

B: You could go to the doctor and get some medicine.

C: You have to go to the hospital! You look like a strawberry!

Below is a list of emergencies. Discuss what you think are good and bad ideas for each situation. Ask a follow-up question about the situation.

Example: Fire

Good idea: You could clear the area and look for a **fire extinguisher**. If you're in a tall building, you shouldn't use the elevator!

Bad idea: You don't have to use the stairs. You should take time to gather all of your belongings – your laptop, your favorite dress, and your stamp collection!

Situation	Good idea	Bad idea
1 Broken arm		
2 Hard drive crash		
3 **Pickpocketed** on vacation		
4 Bank robbery		
5 Allergic reaction		
6 Someone choking		
7 Stuck in the elevator		
8 Car breaks down		
9 Someone drowning		
10 Lost late at night		

fire extinguisher *(n.)*: a device used to stop a fire
pickpocket *(v.)*: to steal something from someone on the street

Discussion Questions

1 When was the last time you had to deal with an emergency situation? Explain what happened.

2 Do you feel that it's safe to walk alone at night? Why or why not?

3 Are you the kind of person who can **keep cool** in an emergency, or do you panic?

4 Have you ever taken a first aid or lifesaving course?
   - If so, what kind of techniques did you learn?
   - Have you ever had to use them?

5 Is your house well-protected in case of fire and robbery?
   - What kinds of precautions have been taken?
   - What kinds of precautions need to be taken?

6 Have you ever been mugged or pickpocketed?
   - What happened?
   - If not, do you know anyone who has?

7 Have you ever seen **an accident waiting to happen**?
   - What was the situation?

8 Have you ever been in a scary situation while traveling?
   - What happened?

an accident waiting to happen *(idiom):* describes a situation that will most likely lead to a problem or accident
keep cool *(idiom):* to remain calm

LESSON 2

>> WARM UP

Objectives:
/ Express unexpected results

A.
1. What is the biggest problem facing your country today?
   > What could you do to fix this problem?
2. What is the biggest problem facing the world today?
   > What could you do to fix this problem?

B. Rank the following problems in order from 1 (most serious) to 5 (least serious)
   > Failing economy
   > Smoking
   > Pollution of the oceans
   > Typhoons
   > Terrorist attacks

A. Expect the Unexpected

Language Point: Expressing an Unexpected Result Using **Even Though** and **Although**

Even though and **Although** express something which is not expected.
▶ *Even though I'm on a diet, I ate an entire chocolate cake.*

◇ Note: Just like sentences with because and since, even though and although can come in the second part of a sentence.
I ate an entire cake even though I'm on a diet.

PART 1 ● Match the phrase on the left with its contrasting idea on the right using **even though** or **although**.

1. Jack studied hard
2. Susan went on a diet
3. Sometimes Lisa feels lonely
4. Grandpa is a **ladies' man**
5. Jack tried to impress his date
6. Richard didn't get the job
7. Mr. Squiggles is hungry

A. He has eaten three times today.
B. He was the most qualified.
C. He failed the exam.
D. She has a lot of friends.
E. She was not interested.
F. He has terrible **fashion sense**.
G. She still gained weight.

Tip
In conversation it is common for speakers to end a sentence with the word **though**.

A: *The weather was cold yesterday.*
B: *Yes it was. I went to the beach though.*

The meaning is: Even though it was cold, I went to the beach.

fashion sense (idiom): understanding of fashion trends
ladies' man (n.): a man who attracts women

PART 2 • Use the given phrase and **even though** or **although** to express an unexpected result.

The temperature was about forty degrees.

> **Example:**
> - We waited in line for tickets **even though** the temperature was about forty degrees.
> - **Although** the temperature was forty degrees, we went out for hot chocolate.

My friend loves smoking.

The weather man said it wouldn't rain.

The road looked safe.

That tiger looks friendly.

My cousin says he saw a UFO.

Nobody was hurt in the earthquake.

It's the middle of May.

There's a trash can in the parking lot.

The guide said the volcano was **dormant**.

dormant *(adj.)*: not active

B. Saving the World, One Idea at a Time...

 Comparatives

What are the good and bad points of each of the ideas below? Discuss the ideas and think of at least one good and bad point for each. Consider:
- Which option is more fun?
- Which option makes a person look better?
- Which option is better for people's health?
- Which option is better for the environment?

PART 1

Consumerism

1. Buying a new car
   - Good point: New cars are comfortable and convenient.
   - Bad point: Driving a car creates pollution. Also, driving in traffic is stressful.
2. Buying new clothes
3. Drinking coffee from disposable cups 
4. Buying a new notebook
5. Buying new shoes whenever a pair wears out 
6. Taking a long shower with hot water every day 
7. Buying new books
8. Getting fruit and vegetables from the grocery store 
9. Updating your smart phone whenever a new model is released

Conservationism

1. Using public transportation
   - Good point: Public transportation makes less pollution than cars.
   - Bad point: Public transportation is crowded. Also, public transportation can be inconvenient if I miss a train or bus and arrive late to work.
2. Buying used clothes or trading clothes with friends
3. Drinking coffee from a reusable coffee cup
4. Making a notebook by stapling together recycled paper 
5. Repairing an old pair of shoes
6. Taking a short shower every day
7. Going to the library 
8. Growing your own fruits and vegetables
9. Using your smart phone until it breaks

PART 2
Now, make sentences contrasting pairs of ideas. Use the good and bad points brainstormed above.

Example:
- *Although driving in traffic is stressful, cars are comfortable and convenient.*
- *Even though public transportation can be inconvenient, it is good for the environment because it makes less pollution than cars.*

---

conservationism *(n.)*: the idea that protecting the environment is beneficial
consumerism *(n.)*: belief in the idea that acquiring goods is positive and beneficial

C. Doomsday, an Activity of Disastrous Proportions

PART 1 ● Discuss the following ways the world might end. How likely is each one? Why do you think so?

How will the world end?

ASTEROID IMPACT

CLIMATE CHANGE

SUPER VIRUS

NUCLEAR WAR

MACHINES TAKE OVER

OTHER

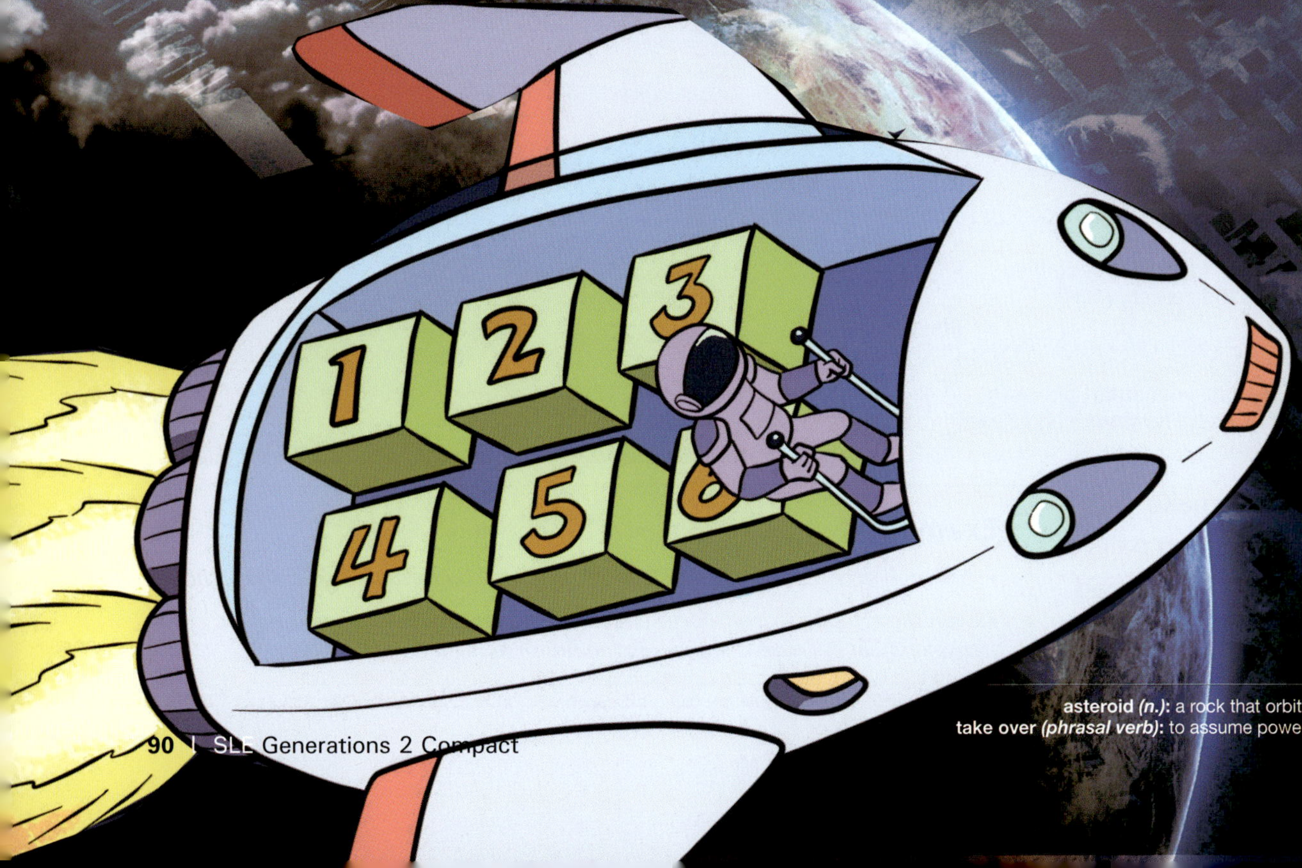

asteroid *(n.)*: a rock that orbits around the sun
take over *(phrasal verb)*: to assume power over something

PART 2 • The world has ended!

- There are only thirteen survivors on the entire planet, one of whom is an astronaut.
- The only way for the human race to continue is to leave Earth on a spaceship.
- The spaceship only fits six people.
- The astronaut must go.
- Of the remaining twelve people, only five can go.

Which five of these people will continue the human race?

Frank
70 years old
Medical Doctor
Very **blunt**

Bonnie
35 years old
Police Officer
Constant **hiccups**

Nicholas
35 years old
Reformed Criminal
Amazing singer

Sophie
31 years old
Lawyer
Compulsive liar

Eleanor
43 years old
Scientist
Scaredy cat

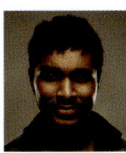
Roberto
30 years old
Farmer
Very quiet

Mark
50 years old
Religious Leader
Perfect memory

Vinny
33 years old
Construction Worker
Excellent with children

Luis
55 years old
Electrician
Excellent writer

Anita
27 years old
Medical Student
Forgetful

Gladys
50 years old
Psychologist
Speaks six languages

Steve
27 years old
Chef
Gambling addiction

blunt *(adj.)*: extremely straightforward with one's words and actions
compulsive *(adj.)*: driven by strong drive to do certain things
hiccups *(n.)*: sound made that effects one's breathing
scaredy cat *(idiom)*: a person who is easily frightened or intimidated

- Likely possibilities
- Should and could for advice

PART 3

After a long journey, the survivors of planet Earth land on their new home planet. You are the astronaut.

> The air is breathable.
> The temperature is very hot.
> The new planet has some plants and small trees, but there is no sign of intelligent life.

Using the people your group selected from Part 2, discuss how they could deal with the following situations.

1. The group needs a leader. Among the survivors from Part 2, who should they choose and why?
2. Several survivors are very depressed. Morale is very low. Nobody wants to do anything.
3. There is a fight between two of the crew members and they refuse to talk to one another.
    - Which two survivors do you think are most likely to get into a fight?
    - What can the group do to solve this problem?
4. The survivors do not want to spend more time inside the spaceship. They need to build shelter on the new planet.
5. There is a strange fungus growing on some of the important equipment. You're not sure if it's safe or dangerous.
    - One of the survivors tries to eat some of the strange fungus and gets very sick.
6. The survivors discover the planet is inhabited by small, furry, rabbit-like animals. What do you do with them?
7. The food supplies are slowly running out. There is a container full of various seeds, but the label is missing.
8. There is something wrong with the solar panels and they are not working well. You will need power if you want to keep using electronic devices.
9. Clothing is slowly wearing out.

Bonus: What are some other issues that you will need to solve in order to continue the human race? What are some possible solutions?

Discussion Questions

1. What is important to do and **watch out** for during or after the following natural disasters:
   - An earthquake?
   - A forest fire?
   - A tsunami?
   - A **tornado**?
   - An avalanche?
   - A **drought**?
   - An **outbreak**?

2. Do you prefer to live carefully, or to **take risks**?
   - Why is it **better to be safe than sorry**?

3. There are some ongoing issues happening in our world every day, such as starvation, poverty, and war.
   - Would you consider these issues to be emergencies? Why or why not?

4. What are some examples of manmade disasters?
   - What could be done to fix these problems?

5. What are some ways we can **reach out** to people who have been affected by disasters?

6. What disasters are possible in your country? Do these things ever worry you?

UNIT 5 REVIEW

How well can you use:
- ☐ Language to express different levels of importance?
- ☐ Even though and although to express unexpected results?

What do you need to study more?

---

better to be safe than sorry *(idiom)*: the idea that one should always try to be careful
drought *(n.)*: a period of water shortage
outbreak *(n.)*: the sudden spread of something such as sickness or conflict
reach out *(phrasal verb)*: help someone in need
take a risk *(idiom)*: to do something without knowing what the result will be
tornado *(n.)*: air that moves over land and leaves destruction on the land that it touches
watch out *(phrasal verb)*: to be alert for a problem or danger

Activity: Create a Superhero

Work with a partner to create a superhero that can solve what you consider to be the most urgent problems in the world today.

Example:
Superhero's name: Woof Woman

Problem that he or she wants to solve: Woof Woman wants to save dogs that live on the streets without a home.

Appearance and costume: Woof Woman wears all black with stylish accessories (such as a hat, necklace, and sunglasses).

Superpower: Woof Woman has a cell phone that barks whenever a dog in distress is nearby. Her cell phone can also communicate with dogs, so dogs can send her text messages expressing their thoughts.

Sidekick: Woof Woman is never seen without her trusty dog, Hubert, by her side.

Enemy: Woof Woman's enemies are thoughtless dog owners everywhere.

PART 1

Superhero's name:	
Problem that he or she wants to solve:	
Appearance and costume:	
Superpower:	
Sidekick:	
Enemy:	

PART 2

What would your superhero do if he or she had to face their enemy?

Example: Woof Woman would talk to thoughtless dog owners about caring for their pets. She would also use her cell phone to share mistreated dogs' opinions about their owners.

What does your superhero do in his or her free time?

Example: Woof Woman likes to shop for dog treats, and sit at outdoor café tables with Hubert.

sidekick (n.): a hero's assistant

The Flood: Moving Forward

By **Leigh King**, PNN

The past several weeks of wet weather have finally taken a toll as a flood submerged the local area last night, leaving two meters of water covering some roads, and leaving residents stranded, unable to return to their homes.

Meteorologists said that the sudden flood was caused by heavy rain even though the spring season is usually dry in this area. Stan Holmes, a local weather man, said, "Such a large amount of rain is unusual for this time of year. We were all surprised that the rain continued for two whole weeks. Hopefully now we'll have sunny weather for the rest of the spring."

The flood has touched many people, some in tragic ways.

"This flood was completely unexpected," said local resident Richard Thompson, "we barely had enough time to grab our most valued possessions before the water began to cover our floors in the house. Although we managed to save our important possessions, we were in such a hurry that we forgot to bring our family cat, Mr. Squiggles, out of the house. Now, we're not sure where he is."

As the families affected by the flood begin to repair their homes and move forward with their lives, they have asked for the support of the local community.

Police deputy Darren Deeds told PNN that although the flooding was sudden, there were no reports of casualties or injuries. "Everyone was able to get out of the neighborhood in an orderly fashion. Being prepared for these kinds of emergencies is the most important thing. I did see the strangest thing, though," Deeds said, "It was a cat floating down the street on a wooden door. He must be well out to sea now."

A. Discussion
1. What caused the flood?
   ▸ Why was the flood unexpected?
2. What kinds of problems do you think that a flood might cause for a community?
   ▸ How can these problems be solved?
3. How can people help each other during or after an emergency such as a fire or flood?

B. Writing
Write a short emergency plan for evacuating your house in case of an emergency such as a flood. Think about:
▸ What would you do before the emergency to prepare?
▸ What steps are important to take during an emergency to be safe?
▸ What would you have to do after the emergency is over?

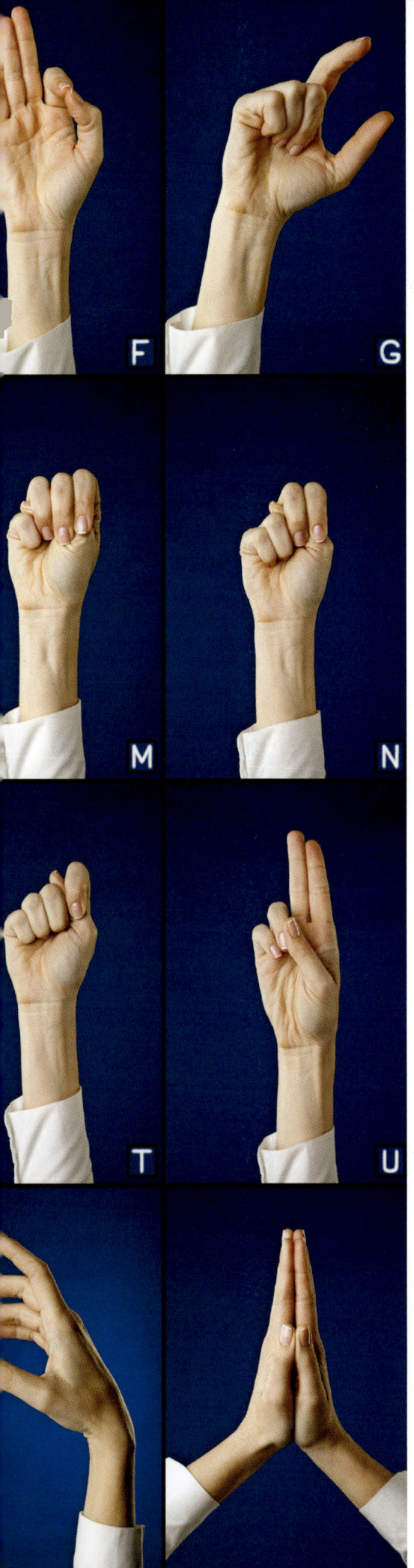

WARM UP

How do you express the following phrases without speaking?

- I don't know.
- Call me.
- It's too loud in here.
- Please sit down.
- I'm thinking.
- I'm scared!
- Follow me.
- Looks delicious.
- You're late.
- I'm tired.
- Great job.
- You're cute.

IDIOMS

- **Poker face**
  No one can see when she's lying because she has an excellent *poker face*.
- **Jump to conclusions**
  I wouldn't *jump to any conclusions* about him just because he doesn't care about fashion.

PHRASAL VERBS

- **Figure out**
  The best way to *figure out* a word you don't know is to explain its use, location, and description to the person you are asking.
- **Get across**
  Sometimes it's difficult to *get your meaning across* with just words.

COLLOCATIONS

- **Make eye contact**
  It is important to *make eye contact* with the interviewer during a job interview.
- **Pass judgment**
  It's not fair to *pass judgment* on her just because of how she looks.

LESSON 1

A. Body Language

PART 1

Discuss what the people are trying to say in each picture and match them with the expressions below. Then discuss when and where you would use the expression.

1. Putting your hand on your forehead
2. Bowing
3. Holding your nose
4. A short hug and sometimes a kiss on the cheek
5. Smiling with your eyes closed
6. Putting your hand in front of you, palm out
7. Bending forward, holding your hands to your stomach
8. Rolling your eyes
9. Putting your hand to your chin
10. Pointing in a direction

a. I'm thinking.
b. Hello. *(informal)*
c. I am content.
d. Something smells bad.
e. I am in pain!
f. Look at that!
g. Nice to meet you. *(formal)*
h. I made a mistake.
i. Stop right there!
j. I'm really not interested in what you're saying.

B. It's Show Time!

Language Point : Making Assumptions

Seems/Looks + adjective expresses opinions about something based on appearance.
- He looks nice because he's wearing a bright-colored shirt and smiling.
- She seems friendly because she's talking to lots of people.

Seems like/Looks like + noun makes an assumption about something based on appearance.
- He looks like the kind of person who cares about his health.
- She seemed like she was lonely when we saw her walking in the park the other day.

Pre-listening

Look at the pictures. Describe what kind of show you think it is.

Listening TRACK 12-13

Which of the television programs did Lisa and Richard see as they were flipping through the channels? Circle the shows that Lisa and Richard talked about. Put a star next to the show that they decided to watch.

Post-listening

1. After listening to Richard and Lisa's conversation, do you feel like your **first impressions** of the shows were correct?
   - How do the people in the pictures look or seem now that you know a bit more about them?
2. Is it fair to judge people based on your first impression?
   - Do you consider yourself a **good judge of character**?

first impression *(idiom)*: the initial opinion of someone
good judge of character *(idiom)*: able to decide whether someone is good or bad easily

C. The Power of First Impressions

PART 1 ● Discuss what impressions Blake and Zoey make based on their appearance, behavior, and choices.

Blake looks friendly because he has a big smile. He looks like a relaxed person because his hair is a bit messy.

Zoey seems like a very serious person because she's not smiling. She looks like a creative person because her hair has an unusual style.

This is them.

Getting dressed in the morning for work

Driving to work

Eating lunch

Talking to a coworker

Taking an evening class
On a date together

PART 2 ● Now consider yourself in each of the above situations.
- How do you act and present yourself?
- What do you think your choices say to others?
- Do you think this is a bad or good thing?

Discussion Questions

1 Why do you think we use body language to communicate?
- ▶ If people did not use body language, how would this affect communication?

2 A friend of yours from another country is coming to visit you. What kind of body language shouldn't they use?

3 How important is it to understand the gestures and body language of other cultures?
- ▶ How has body language helped you while traveling in other countries?

4 Is it important to make eye contact with someone when speaking?
- ▶ What kind of judgment would you pass on someone who uses too much eye contact?

5 Do you use your hands to gesture while you are speaking?
- ▶ What miscommunications can happen when not using body language?

6 Do you **jump to conclusions** based on how someone is dressed?
- ▶ How important is our choice of clothing and accessories to how other people see us?

7 How does the face you show the world affect your chances of success?
- ▶ Is it more important to show the world you are a happy or serious person?

8 What kind of body language indicates that a person is lying?
- ▶ Do you have a good **poker face**?

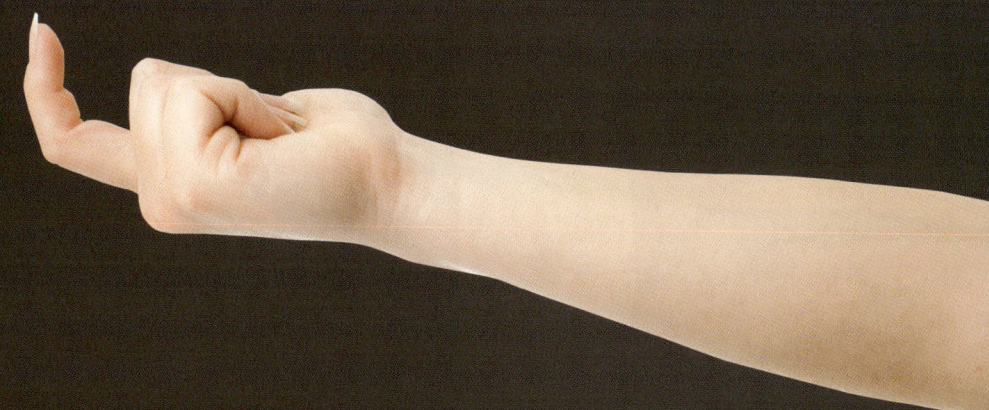

jump to conclusions *(idiom):* to make a quick decision
poker face *(idiom):* a face that expresses no emotion

LESSON 2

>> WARM UP

Objectives:
/ Describing what kind or which one

A. If you don't know a vocabulary word in English, what is the best way to find out its meaning?

B. Below are sections of larger photographs. Decide what the thing in the picture is.
- What purpose(s) does it have?
- Where is it found?
- What does it look like?

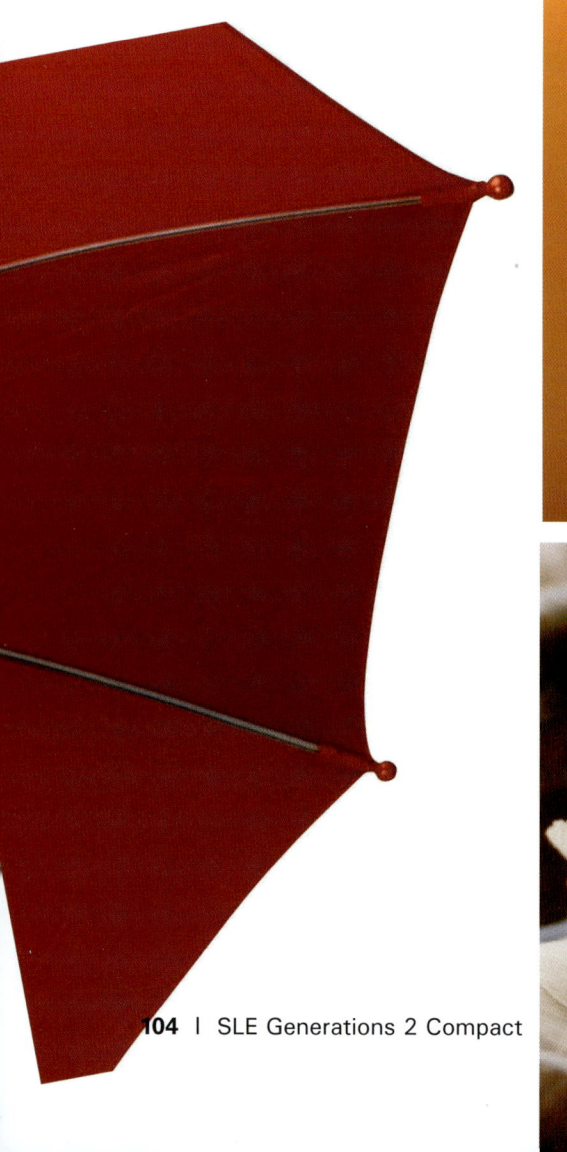

A. It's a Thing-a-ma-bob.

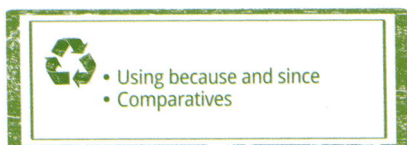
- Using because and since
- Comparatives

A: *She's so cute!*
B: *Which one?*
A: *The girl who is wearing the red dress and the black hat.*
B: *They're both wearing a red dress and a black hat.*
A: *The girl that's on the left.*
B: *I disagree. The girl that's on the right is cuter.*

Language Point: Describing "What Kind" or "Which One"

Who, **Which**, and **That** are relative pronouns that can be used to give more information about a non-specific noun.

Who or That- are used to describe or define a person.
▸ I met a man. What kind of man was he?
▸ I met a man **who** plays the flute. I met a man **that** likes kittens.

Which or That- are used to describe or define a thing.
▸ The man had a flute **which** he played when he walked.
▸ It was a magic flute **that** made kittens follow him around.

PART 1 ● Read the sentences and ask the question. Use **"the"** to make the general noun specific and use **"who, which, or that"** to describe it. Then ask your partner(s) their opinion.

Example:
One day is hot and sunny. Another day is cool and rainy.
▸ Which day do you prefer? Why?
 *I prefer **the** day **that** is cool and rainy because I really hate sweating. How about you?*

1. One student studied until 4 a.m. Another student went to bed at 11 p.m.
   ▸ Who did better on the test? Why?
2. One car is very fast and expensive. Another car uses very little gas and is also expensive.
   ▸ Which car would you choose? Why?
3. One restaurant across the street sells greasy burgers and soda. Another restaurant across the street sells salads and fruit juice.
   ▸ Which restaurant is better? Why?
4. Movie A has a lot of blood and violence. Movie B has a lot of kissing and talking.
   ▸ Which movie is more entertaining? Why?
5. One city has a lot of beautiful old buildings, museums, and rainy weather. Another city has great food, shopping, and really hot weather.
   ▸ Which is better for a vacation? Why?
6. A woman who has a very stressful job spent the weekend sleeping. Another woman who has a very stressful job spent the weekend enjoying her hobbies.
   ▸ Who felt more relaxed after the weekend? Why?

PART 2

Choose a person and describe their profession using *who* or *that*. Guess who it is by the clues given and ask a follow-up question about the person's job.

> **Example:**
> **A:** *This is someone who wears big shoes, a red nose, and makes children laugh.*
> **B:** *You're thinking about a clown. Do you like clowns?*
> **A:** *Actually, I find them terrifying.*

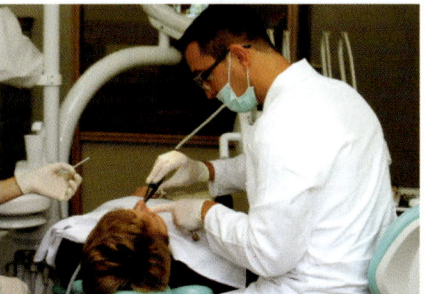

B. Forbidden Words

CAUTION
- Try to get your partner to guess the words/phrases pictured below.
- DO NOT say any of the forbidden words.
- Also, do not use any proper nouns (names of companies, people, holidays or places) in your descriptions.

Example:
A: *This is a thing that you have around 1 P.M. to give you energy.*
B: *Coffee?*
A: *No, not coffee. This is a thing that is similar to dinner or breakfast.*
B: *Oh, I know! Lunch!*
A: *Yes, lunch is correct.*

STUDENT A

Lunch
Forbidden: eat, meal, afternoon

Air Conditioner
Forbidden: summer, cool, classroom, heater

Tape
Forbidden: plastic, clear, office

Coffee
Forbidden: drink, café, brown, bean

Spaceship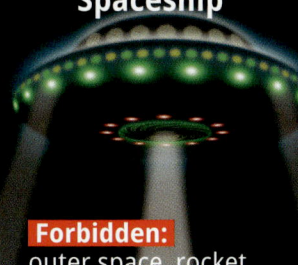
Forbidden: outer space, rocket

Song
Forbidden: voice, sing, concert

Joy
Forbidden: happy, feeling, smile

Tennis Racket
Forbidden: tennis, sport, play

Puppy
Forbidden: baby, dog, small

Flower
Forbidden: plant, pretty, grow

Wheel
Forbidden: circle, bike, car, spin

Music
Forbidden: listen, hear, notes, play

CAUTION

- Try to get your partner to guess the words/phrases pictured below.
- DO NOT say any of the forbidden words.
- Also, do not use any proper nouns (names of companies, people, holidays or places) in your descriptions.

Example:
B: *This is a thing that you might do when you're bored. You wear sneakers to do this.*
A: *Hmmm…walking?*
B: *No…this is a thing that you do in a gym. You use something that is orange and black to do this.*
A: *Oh! Basketball!*
B: *That's right!*

STUDENT B

Basketball

Forbidden: ball, play, sport, athlete

Star

Forbidden: sky, night, bright, sun

Gum

Forbidden: chew, candy

Truck

Forbidden: drive, road, dump

Map

Forbidden: guide, find, lost, tourist

Math
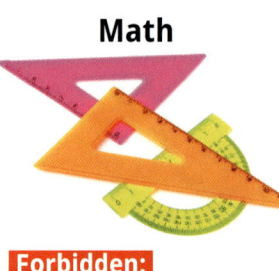
Forbidden: calculator, number, school, test

Plate

Forbidden: eat, meal, dish, food

Dance

Forbidden: move, music, hip hop, ballet

Strawberry

Forbidden: fruit, eat, red, sweet

Sky

Forbidden: blue, cloud, sun

Love

Forbidden: feeling, romantic, boyfriend, girlfriend

Party
Forbidden: celebrate, music, dance

CAUTION

- Try to get your partner to guess the words/phrases pictured below.
- DO NOT say any of the forbidden words.
- Also, do not use any proper nouns (names of companies, people, holidays or places) in your descriptions.

Example:
C: *This is a thing that you might do when you're bored. You do this with your eyes.*
B: *Watching a movie?*
C: *No. This is something sort of like that, but you do this at home.*
B: *Watching television!*
C: *Right! Television is the answer!*

STUDENT C

Television

Forbidden: remote, watch, program, show

Coat

Forbidden: warm, winter, jacket, clothing

Motorcycle

Forbidden: ride, wheel

Sneaker

Forbidden: sport, run, basketball

Subway
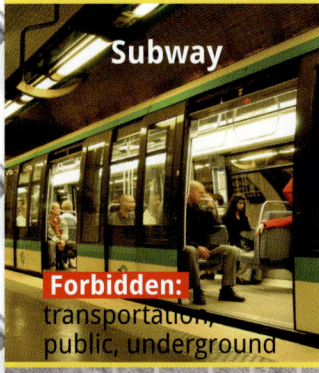
Forbidden: transportation, public, underground

Jeans

Forbidden: pants, clothing, denim, blue

Movie

Forbidden: watch, theater, actor, popcorn

Computer

Forbidden: technology, laptop, type

Winter

Forbidden: cold, snow, ice, season

Sock

Forbidden: shoe, foot, warm, wear

Book

Forbidden: read, paper, study, school

Video Game

Forbidden: play, television, character

Unit 6 You Don't Say | 109

C. Hello, My Name is Dave.

You are a judge at the…

19th Annual
Dave Convention

…and every Dave is invited.

PART 1 •

As the judge, choose the recipient for the following Dave Awards and explain your decision:

MOST AND LEAST / BEST AND WORST

- ✯ Most and Least Exciting
- ✯ Most and Least **Reliable**
- ✯ Most and Least Professional
- ✯ Best Dave
- ✯ Worst Dave
- ✯ Dave You Would Most Likely…

  - Want to Be Friends With
  - Ask for Help
  - Avoid Talking to on the Street
  - Hire for Your Company

Make Up Your Own Awards:
1. _____
2. _____

Example:
A: *I think the award for the most lazy Dave should go to the Dave who is yawning.*
B: *I disagree. I think it should go to the Dave that is not wearing a shirt. He was too lazy to put one on!*

reliable *(adj.):* someone or something that is there when you need it

PART 2 ● **These Are the Daves I Know**

Step 1 Choose a Dave from the previous page, but don't tell anyone who you chose.

Step 2 Take turns asking each other questions in order to find out which Dave everyone chose. You should answer your questions as if you were that Dave. You will have twenty seconds before you must switch to questioning another Dave.

> **Student A:** *Hello, Dave.*
> **Student B:** *Hi, Dave. So, do you enjoy playing sports?*
> **Student A:** *Not really, Dave. Sports are a lot of work.*
> **Student B:** *Really?*
> **Student A:** *Yeah, I prefer relaxing. Do you like movies?*
> **Student B:** *I guess so. As long as they're not too scary.*
>
> **SWITCH!**
>
> **Student B:** *Hey, Dave! What is your favorite hobby?*
> **Student C:** *I really like walking in the woods…*

Step 3 After several minutes, come back together as a class and guess which Dave each person was.

> **Student A:** *He seemed really lazy.*
> **Student C:** *I agree. He didn't want to do anything!*
> **Student A:** *I think is he the Dave that is yawning on the stage.*
> **Student B:** *That's right! I am!*

Alternate rule: Write down a Dave on a small piece of paper and hand it to someone else in the class. That person cannot look at who they are, but everyone else should be able to see the name on the paper. Then ask that person questions based on the piece of paper until that person figures out who they are.

Discussion Questions

1. Have you ever been in a situation when you couldn't remember the word for what you wanted to say?
   - How did you resolve the situation?
   - How do you **get your meaning across** if you don't know how to say something in English?

2. How can you **figure out** a vocabulary word without using a dictionary?
   - Can you describe something's location, use, and appearance?

3. How important is it to know a lot of vocabulary when communicating with a native speaker of another language?
   - Why do you think so?

4. What kind of people bother you?
   - What are your pet peeves? *I am bothered by people who...*

5. What is an ideal friend like? *An ideal friend is someone who...*

6. What kind of movies do you like? *I like movies that...*

7. What would your dream job be? *I want a job that...*

8. What is the best kind of vacation? *I like vacations that...*

UNIT 6 REVIEW

How well can you use:
- ☐ Language to correct information?
- ☐ Who, which, or that to describe or define things and people?

What do you need to study more?

figure out *(phrasal verb)*: to make sense of, to resolve
get across *(phrasal verb)*: to communicate or express information

Activity : Charades

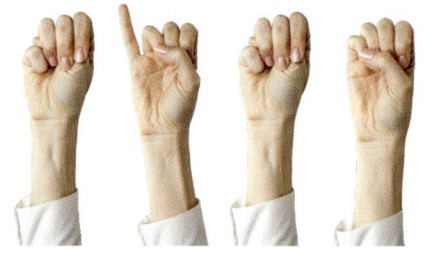

1. Below is a list of categories. Work with your whole class to create a gesture for each category.
2. Choose a category and mime the gesture for that category.
3. Think of a word or phrase related to that category that you can mime. There are a few examples below.
4. Mime the word or phrase that you chose until someone in the class says the word.
   • Optional: To give an extra clue, hold up a finger for every word you are miming.
5. Whoever says your word repeats steps 2-4 with his or her own word or phrase!
   The student who guesses the most words by the end of the game wins!

Animals
• Cat
• Ride a horse

Transportation
• Taxi
• Drive a bus

Movies
• Popcorn
• Watch a sad movie

Travel
• Souvenir
• Climb a mountain

Hobbies
• Tennis
• Shop for new shoes

Food
• Apple
• Eat a slice of pizza

Segue

channel 35
Happy Family 8 p.m.
Follow Steve and Janet Smith and their three children through the ups and downs of life in this popular family drama. In tonight's episode Steve, who is a doctor, will deal with the challenges of Take Your Child to Work Day. His 10-year-old daughter, Annie, will accompany him to the hospital. Annie, who hopes to become a doctor someday, will befriend a patient and learn some valuable lessons about life, medicine, and her father's love.

channel 32
Daily Gag Report 8 p.m.
The top news of the day, presented by hit comedian Joey Jokeson and his cast. Tonight's episode will include interviews with people who own successful cafes, as well as a musical performance by hit band, the Crimson Kings.

channel 38
Socal Life 8 p.m.
Life is never boring in the city of Socal! Watch the real-life adventures of a group of high school students. In tonight's episode, Farah, who is planning the high school's Spring Sunny Dance, will struggle to balance planning the dance, finding the perfect dress, and finding a date to the event. Farah's friend Natalia, who is a member of the school orchestra, will try to help Farah do it all.

channel 47
Cool Science 8 p.m.
Science for people who live in the real world! Tonight, Scientist James Block, a Jacobson Research Fellow from Smithson University presents his current research into safe car technology and the effect that it will have on your life. Learn valuable tips about how to make your current car safer.

channel 50
Law and Justice 8 p.m.
Follow detectives from the Songtown crime lab as they investigate local incidents in this hit crime drama. This evening's episode will follow the detective team as they search for Sandra Patel, a famous artist who was about to unveil an exhibit of paintings at the museum. Detective Gomez, who is preparing to retire from her job with the team, will begin to say goodbye and remember her time working in Songtown.

A. Discussion
1. Which of the television shows on this page would you most likely watch? Why?
   ▶ Which of the television shows on this page would you least likely watch?
2. What kinds of shows do you prefer to watch?

B. Writing
Write a summary like those above describing an episode of your favorite television show.

07
Coulda, Woulda, Shoulda

Past Speculations and Regrets

Objectives:
/ Speculate about the past
/ Listen to a story about travel

WARM UP

What happened in the picture?
Was his team winning or losing?
How do you know?

IDIOMS

- **What's done is done.**
  I would like to go back to college and change my major, but *what's done is done*.
- **Hindsight is 20/20.**
  I wish I hadn't quit my last job. It was better than the job I have now. I guess *hindsight is 20/20*.

PHRASAL VERBS

- **Look back on**
  When I get older, I'll *look back on* this time as the best of my life.
- **Chew over**
  I shouldn't spend so much time *chewing over* my mistake. I can't change what I've done.

COLLOCATIONS

- **No regrets**
  I have *no regrets* about my time living abroad.
- **Guess about**
  I can only make a *guess about* what happened to my car. I parked it right here.

Unit 7 Coulda, Woulda, Shoulda | 117

LESSON 1

A. Who Stole the Cookie from the Cookie Jar?

Language Point : Speculate About the Past

LESS CERTAIN

MORE CERTAIN

Who stole the cookie from the cookie jar?

Positive: **Might/Could** + have + past participle
Jack could have eaten the cookies.

Must + have + past participle
Jack must have eaten the cookies.

Negative: **Might not** + have + past participle
Jack might not have eaten the cookies.

Must not/ Could not + have + past participle
Jack couldn't have eaten the cookies.

speculate *(v.)*: to make a guess about something

Look at the pictures below and answer the questions with a guess. Give a reason why you think so.

> **Example:**
> Charles and Martha are not talking to each other.
>
> **A:** *They **might have had** an argument about what to do on vacation.*
> ▶ They are standing in a long line to get into a restaurant.
>
> **B:** *Charles **must have** forgotten to make a reservation!*

1. Richard and Susan on a cruise
- Where did the cruise go?
- Did anything go wrong?
- The cruise had many activities, including diving, water skiing, gambling, and ballroom dancing. Which activities did they enjoy?
- Susan said she wanted to do something exciting. What did they try?
- They stopped on an island to sightsee. What did they forget to do?
- Where did they get the **lifeboat**?
- How long were they out to sea?

2. Lisa and Biff on vacation
- Where in the world were they?
- What were they looking for?
- What activities did they enjoy?
- Could they speak the language?
- How was the weather?
- Did they go out to a fancy dinner?
- Did they enjoy the food on vacation?

3. Jack on a date
- What kind of restaurant did he meet his date at?
- What food did they order?
- Was he late? Why?
- Where was he?
- Jack gave her flowers and she started crying. Why?
- He told her she looked "interesting" in her outfit. How did she react?
- She said she was going to the restroom and didn't return. Where did she go?

lifeboat *(n.)*: a small boat that is kept on a larger boat in case of emergencies

B. Squiggles' Quest

Pre-listening

Mr. Squiggles has been missing ever since the flood! Look at the map and guess where Mr. Squiggles might have gone by matching each photo to a location on the map.

Listening TRACK 14-15

Now listen to the dialogue and find out where Mr. Squiggles went.

Post-listening

Choose a place that you have been to or a place you want to visit. Your partner needs to ask yes/no questions to figure out which place you've selected.

Example:

A: *Is this a place that is cold?*

B: *Actually, no. This is a place that is very warm.*

A: *Are there deserts there?*

B: *Lots of them.*

A: *You **might have gone** to Egypt.*

B: *Yes!*

A: *Wow, really, have you been to Egypt?*

B: *Yes, when I was a teenager, I...*

Post-listening

Based on what you see in the following suitcases:
Where do you think the owner went?
What did they do there?
Why do you think so?

Unit 7 Coulda, Woulda, Shoulda | 123

C. The Graphs of Life

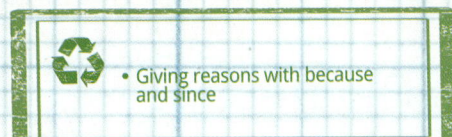
- Giving reasons with because and since

PART 1 ● Based on the information given in the graphs below, speculate about what could have happened in each situation.

James and Sue's Blind Date

James and Sue went on a blind date. They met at a restaurant at 7 P.M.
Based on their feelings, try to decide what might have happened during the date.

> **A:** *James might have been disappointed at the beginning of the date because Sue was late. She must have looked beautiful, though, because James was ecstatic when he met her.*
>
> **B:** *Sue was happy at the beginning of the date. She could have started to feel unhappy when she met him because he didn't bring any flowers.*

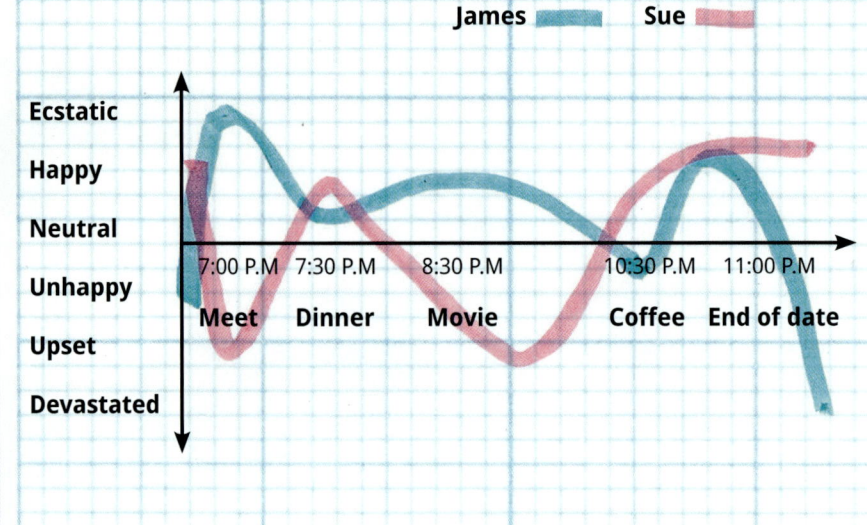

Alex's Life

Alex was 20 years old in the year 2000.
Based on the feelings shown in the graph, try to decide when the life events in the box might have occurred.

Life Events
- Get a new job
- Fail an important test
- Break up with a girlfriend
- Discover a new hobby
- Move to a new city
- Get married
- Make a mistake
- Lose something important

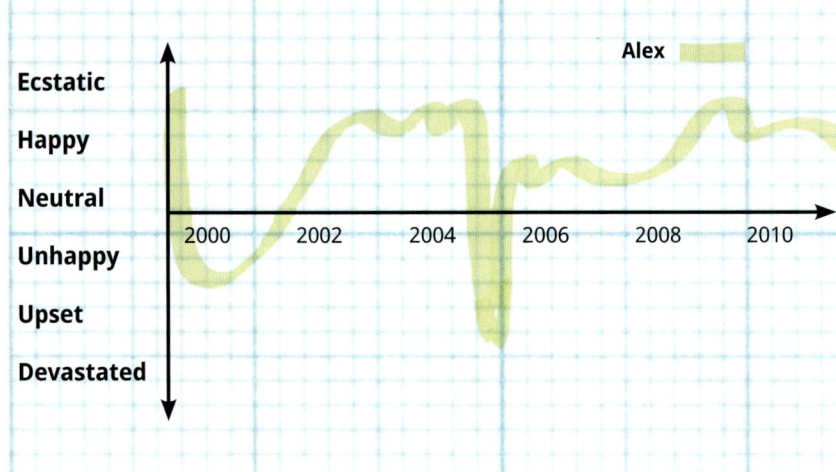

PART 2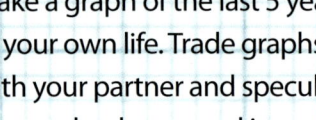
Make a graph of the last 5 years of your own life. Trade graphs with your partner and speculate about what happened in each of your lives.

Discussion Questions

1 Do you like TV shows that are about unsolved mysteries?
- ▶ Do you think you would be a good detective? Why or Why not?
- ▶ Does your country have any famous mysteries? What do you think happened?

2 Has anything ever **slipped your mind**?
- ▶ What do you think might have happened?

3 Can you make some guesses about what your SLE instructor was like in high school?

4 Have you ever lost something and not been able to find it?
- ▶ What do you think might have happened to it?

5 What do you think the rest of your classmates did last weekend?
- ▶ Why do you think they enjoy these things?

6 Why has English become one the most widely spoken languages in the world?

7 Can you recall any strange or unexplained events in your life?
- ▶ What do you think the explanation might be?

slip one's mind *(idiom)*: to forget about something

LESSON 2

>> WARM UP

Objectives:
/ Express regrets

What do you wish was different about…
…public transportation?
…education?
…your city?
…your country?

A. Coulda, Shoulda, Woulda but Didn't.

Language Point : Expressing Regret and Advice in the Past

Should + Have + Past Participle expresses...

...regret about something you did.
- I **should've brought** an umbrella.
- I **shouldn't have** said that. I think I gave away the surprise.

...advice about something a person did or did not do (**hindsight** advice).
- He **shouldn't have said** that. She looks angry with him.

Could + Have + Past Participle expresses choices that were not made.
- You **could've bought** an umbrella at the subway station or **borrowed** one from your coworker.
◇ Note: 'Could have' is not used in the negative to express regret.

Look at the pictures below and think about what things the person(s) **shouldn't have done** and what they **could have done** differently.

Example: Randall

A: He shouldn't have gotten a tattoo! He's too young.

B: He could have waited until he was older. His mom is going to kill him.

C: He could have just sent some flowers to the girl he wants to impress.

Darla

Reggie

Penny

Agatha and Angie

Bonny and Clyde

hindsight *(n.)*: the understanding gained after an incident has occurred

B. Life Coach

PART 1

> Imagine that you are in one of the situations below.
> Ask your partner what you could have or should have done differently.
> Give advice on what your partner should have done and what they could do in the future.

 • Giving advice with could and should

Example:

A: *I got into a big argument with my coworker. After the argument, I found out that she's been really sick recently. I feel terrible! What **could I have done** differently?*

B: *You **shouldn't have gotten** into an argument so quickly. You could have tried to talk to her.*

- Your boyfriend or girlfriend went away to military service.
- Now, you don't know if you can wait for him or her to come back.

- You bought a used computer one month ago from a friend for $500.
- A month after you bought the computer, it stopped working.
- The computer needs $450 worth of repairs.

- You are working on a project with your friend.
- You've been so busy that you haven't even started it yet.
- Your friend is upset because she had to work all night to finish the project alone.

- Your best friend has a terrible voice but thinks his voice is fantastic.
- When he asked about it, you told him his voice was "unique".
- Lately, he has been talking about trying to start a career as a pop star.

- One of your coworkers has been grumpy recently.
- You got into an argument and said some unkind things to him.
- You found out that he has been dealing with serious health issues.

- Your parents have always dreamed that you would become a doctor.
- You are in medical school now, but you hate it.
- You want to quit, but don't know what to say to your parents.

- You are attending university in the United States.
- Your parents gave you enough money for the entire year.
- You wasted all of the money on a gambling trip in Las Vegas.

- You've been working for the last five years.
- You go out several times a week with friends.
- You haven't managed to save any money, and now you want to buy a house.

- You are in love with an incredible man/woman who you see every day on the bus.
- You've never talked to this person, so he/she doesn't even know who you are.

C. Choices and Consequences

PART 1 ● For each situation below, discuss which choice you would make and why. Use the boxes to keep track of your answers.

> **Example:**
> *I would keep the money because I'm not responsible for the waiter's mistakes.*

1 At a restaurant, your waiter does not charge you for part of your meal.

Would you
- a. let the waiter know about the mistake and give him the money back? ☐
- b. keep the money? ☐

2 You come across a young girl looking at a beautiful dress in a store window. You have a coupon for one free outfit.

Would you
- a. give the girl your coupon so she can get the dress? ☐
- b. get yourself a very stylish outfit? ☐

3 You get to the bus stop a few seconds too late. The bus driver looks at you and smiles as he drives away.

Would you
- a. wait patiently for the next bus? ☐
- b. run after the bus, yelling and making rude gestures? ☐

4 You arrive at your favorite restaurant for lunch. A very hungry looking dog is sitting by the door looking at you. You only have a little money.

Would you
- a. feed the dog? ☐
- b. feed yourself? ☐

5 You worked very late last night and got very little sleep. You're absolutely exhausted. You know your boss is out of the office today.

Would you
- a. sleep in and be late to work, but well rested? ☐
- b. force yourself to go to work on time? ☐

6 You have to buy a new phone. You've put yourself on a budget so you can go on vacation.

Would you
- a. buy the cheap phone that can only make phone calls and text for $15 a month? ☐
- b. buy the expensive phone with lots of games and apps for $100 a month? ☐

Unit 7 Coulda, Woulda, Shoulda | 129

PART 2

> Look at the **consequences** of the decisions you made in Part 1.
> After you find out the consequences, discuss whether you regret your decision or not.
> If so, what could you have done differently?

> **Example:**
> I would keep the money because I'm not responsible for the waiter's mistakes.
> **A:** *The waiter loses his job. Do you regret your decision?*
> **B:** *That's really terrible. I guess I could've been honest and given back the money.*
> **C:** *I wouldn't regret it. He should've been more careful. It's his job.*

1 ▶
a. The waiter thanks you for your honesty and gives you a coupon for a free meal.
b. Later that night, the waiter's boss accuses him of stealing. He is fired.

2 ▶
a. The girl thanks you for the coupon. She goes inside and buys her boyfriend a jacket.
b. You wear your stylish outfit out to dinner. You spill wine on it. The outfit is ruined.

3 ▶
a. It starts to rain while you wait for the next bus, and you don't have an umbrella.
b. You trip in the street from running. Everyone laughs at you as the bus drives away.

4 ▶
a. The dog is so happy about the food that he starts following you everywhere.
b. You see the dog outside the restaurant for a few days. After a week, the dog disappears.

5 ▶
a. Your boss came to work today! He yells at you for being two hours late.
b. You make your afternoon presentation but make lots of mistakes because you're so tired.

6 ▶
a. You feel you're missing out on a bit of your social life, but you manage to save enough to go on vacation for a month.
b. When you go to buy travel tickets, you realize you don't have enough money. Instead of traveling overseas, you have to spend your vacation at home.

consequence *(n.)*: result

Discussion Questions

1 If you could go back in time and change one thing about your life, what would it be?

> ▶ Why do you think changing this thing would make a big difference to your life?

2 What are three things about your present situation that you would like to change?

3 Which bad habits do you have, and how have you tried to change them?

4 Who is someone you admire for having made positive changes in his/her life?

5 Can you **look back on** a moment in your life when you said something you probably shouldn't have said?

> ▶ When was it?
>
> ▶ Why did you say it?

6 Do you feel like you should have taken high school or university more seriously or less seriously? Why?

Activity: The Pie of Regret

Think of an answer for each of the following things…..

1 Something you should have remembered but forgot _____

2 Something you shouldn't have eaten _____

3 Something you shouldn't have bought _____

4 A day you should have stayed in bed _____

5 A place you shouldn't have gone _____

- Now, imagine that the pie below is the total amount of your regret.
- Divide the pie into pieces with an approximate percentage for each of the above things.
- Then discuss what you regret more and why.

- Vague and precise language
- Giving reasons with because and since

Example:

A: *What is something you shouldn't have eaten?*

B: *I shouldn't have eaten an entire pizza by myself when I was in university because it made me really sick.*

A: *Is that your biggest slice of regret?*

B: *No. It's only around twenty percent. I regret buying these shoes at full price a lot more.*

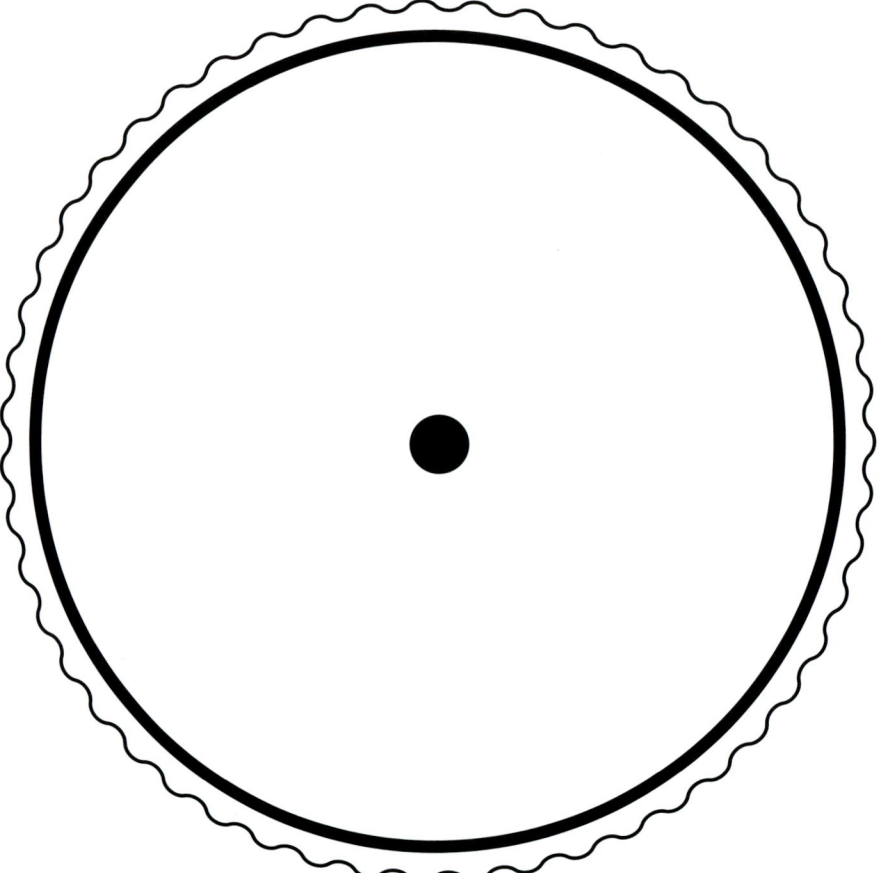

Where in the World is Mr. Squiggles?

May 10th
Buenos dias. I live in Barcelona, Spain. One day a cat came floating up to the beach on a door! He seemed quite hungry, so I took him to a café where we ate tapas. We met a photographer who said he wanted to take his picture and disappeared after that. He could have gone away with the photographer.

May 25th
Ahh yes. Good old Mr. Squiggles! I met him in a bar in Spain. On a photo shoot in Kenya we were surprised by a big lion in a tree. I thought I was done for, but Mr. Squiggles chased the lion off! I lost him after that. I heard a rumor he might have been on plane bound for Asia.

May 29th
Sawatdee. I'm an elephant veterinarian. I met this Mr. Squiggles in Thailand, where he helped us care for sick elephants. I'm not sure where he is, though. He seemed to be very friendly with a tourist who was visiting. He must have left with her.

June 10th
G'day! I met old Squiggles while on holiday. He came back to Australia with me. I told my brother about his ability to communicate with elephants and he decided to take him to Antarctica where he is doing research on penguins.

June 19th
Hola. I am a scientist from Argentina. I met this cat on the Antarctic ice where he was doing an amazing penguin mating dance! I decided to introduce him to my cousin, who is a dancer in Brazil.

June 25th
Tudo bon. I danced Samba with the Squiggles. He was the most talented dancing cat I have ever worked with. I took him with me on a tour of the United States, but he disappeared. I think he might have been kidnapped!

June 30th
Howdy! We were on vacation in Hollywood when we saw this cat. My friend Darla told me he was an internet celebrity. So we grabbed him to get a photo in front of the Hollywood sign. He ran off though! He must have been scared.

A. Discussion
1. Would you like to travel to any of the places mentioned on the blog?
   - If you could travel around the world for two months, where would you go?
2. How do you think Mr. Squiggles might have traveled from one location to the next?

B. Writing
Write a short blog posting like the ones above saying you have seen Mr. Squiggles in your country and guess what you think might have happened to him.

WARM UP

Do you agree or disagree with the following statements? Why or why not?

- The older you are the easier it is to get left behind by technology.
- Handwritten letters are pointless.
- We are currently living in the greatest period of change in history.
- Newer is always better.

IDIOMS

- **Behind the times**
  My dad is really *behind the times*. He's been using the same cell phone for twelve years.
- **Cutting-edge**
  I heard she got a job with a really *cutting-edge* tech company.

PHRASAL VERBS

- **Keep up**
- **Fall behind**
  The software updates are so fast these days that it's really hard to *keep up*. I've *fallen behind* recently.

COLLOCATIONS

- **Computer illiterate**
  My grandmother is *computer illiterate*. She has no idea what email even is.
- **Tech-savvy**
  My grandfather, on the other hand, is really *tech-savvy*. He even builds his own robots.

Unit 8 The Future is Now | 135

LESSON 1

A. What's Old is New

- Comparatives and superlatives
- Advice with could and should

STUDENT A
Film Camera
Word Processor
Landline Phone
Handwritten Letters
Satellite/Cable TV
Microwave
Map and Compass
Text Messaging
CD Player
Books

PART 1

You and your partner are both using different types of technology. One of you is using **outdated** technology, and the other is using cutting-edge technology. In each case, try to explain to your partner why your type of technology is better, and persuade your partner to use the same technology as you.

> **Example:**
> **A:** *Film cameras are better than digital cameras because they allow you to be more creative.*
> **B:** *No, I think digital cameras are easier to use because they allow you to take as many pictures as necessary to get a good photo. Film is expensive! You should definitely buy a digital camera.*

STUDENT B
Digital Camera
Typewriter
Mobile Phone
Email
TV on a Smart Phone/Tablet
Oven
Navigation System/GPS
Talking on the Phone
MP3 Player
E-Books

outdated *(adj.)*: behind current trends

B. Postmodern Prometheus

Pre-listening
- In what jobs have people been replaced by machines?
- Look at the picture and make a prediction about what kinds of things you think the robot can do.

Listening TRACK 16-17

Grandpa Charles built a robot! Find out what it can do!

Post-listening

1. What three things does Grandpa say he has built the robot to do?

2. If you could build your own robot, what would it be able to do?

3. Do you know about any robots that are in use today? How are they used?

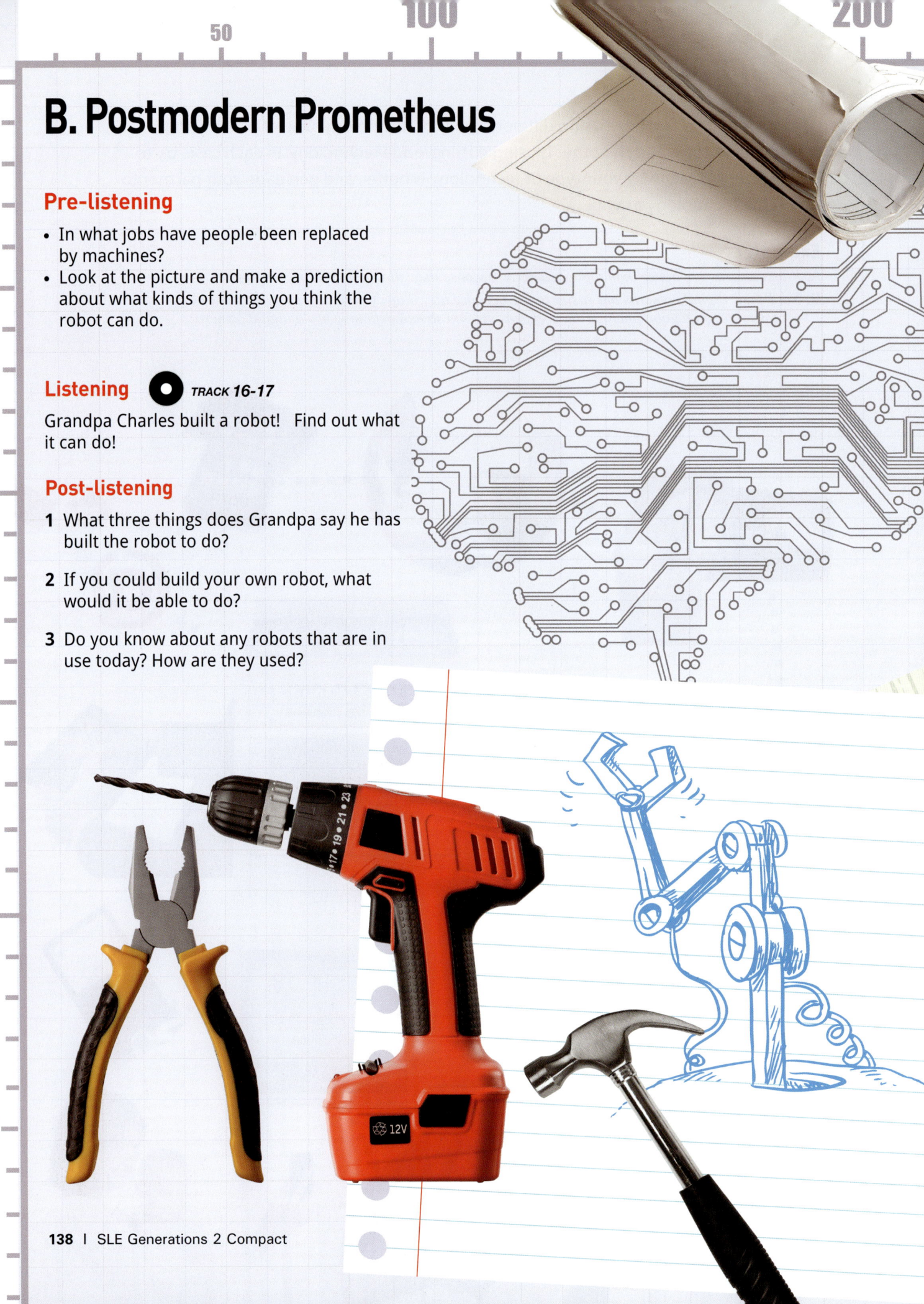

Unit 8 The Future is Now | 139

C. Robot Schmobot

PART 1 ● You have been given a very special opportunity! The JudsoCo Corporation™ has developed their first **humanoid** robot for personal home use. You have been selected to test out this robot, but first they want to know what kind of robot would be most useful to you.

Step 1
Functions. Below are a series of possible functions, but due to space and cost, only some can be put into your robot. A standard function is 1 point. An **upgraded** function is 3 points. Choose as many functions as you want up to a total of 10 points.

Example:
- *I want my robot to act as a life coach because I need someone to help me prepare for job interviews.*
- *I'd also like it if the robot could run errands and do all of my cleaning and laundry so I can have more free time to prepare for interviews.*
- *Finally, I want my robot to be able to give me a comforting hug because I need to get more hugs.*

STANDARD (1 point)
—————————————
UPGRADE (3 points)

1

"May I help you?"

Standard ☐
The robot has limited speaking ability. It can use and understand 10 pre-programmed words.

Upgrade ☐
The robot has a vocabulary of 10,000 words.

2

Standard ☐
When you are not home, the robot can send the police a message if a **burglar** tries to enter.

Upgrade ☐
The robot will defend the home from **intruders**.

3

Standard ☐
The robot can make toast and coffee in the morning.

Upgrade ☐
The robot is a master cook and can create any meal you ask for.

4

Standard ☐
The robot can answer and open the front door.

Upgrade ☐
The robot can run **errands** for you.

---

humanoid *(adj.)*: having the appearance or characteristics of a human
intruder *(n.)*: someone who enters without permission
burglar *(n.)*: someone who enters a building illegally with the intent of stealing something
errand *(n.)*: a short trip with a clear goal or mission
upgrade *(v.)*: to improve

5

Standard ☐
The robot can give you a comforting hug.

Upgrade ☐
The robot can give you an excellent massage.

6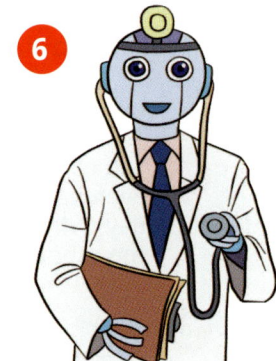

Standard ☐
The robot can **diagnose** minor health issues.

Upgrade ☐
The robot can **treat** minor health issues.

7

Standard ☐
The robot can give you fashion and style advice.

Upgrade ☐
The robot can act as a life coach and **therapist**.

8

Standard ☐
The robot can vacuum and clean up spills.

Upgrade ☐
The robot can do all of the cleaning and laundry in the house.

Step 2

Select the appearance. Below are four possible body types. Discuss the pros and cons of the appearance of each. Which do you prefer and why?

Step 3

Name your robot.

Step 4

Present your robot!

My robot's name is......

---

diagnose *(v.)*: to determine the type of illness that someone has
therapist *(n.)*: someone who specializes in particular form of treatment
treat *(v.)*: to deal with or care for an illness or injury

PART 2

You have had the robot for a few weeks. Below are a series of situations that have occurred in that time. Discuss how you and the robot you designed would handle the situations below.

1. You wake up and get ready for your day. What will you ask the robot to do?

2. You come home in the evening after a long day. What will you ask the robot to do?

3. You had a bad day. You got in a fight with your best friend.

4. You have an opportunity for a new job or promotion.

5. You've invited someone special to your house for a hot date. You really want to impress them.

6. It's late at night, and you hear someone break in.

7. You've been feeling feverish for a few days now. You've been really stressed with a few life issues, and you're not sure if that's causing it.

8. You are going on vacation for two weeks. What will you ask the robot to do while you are gone?

Post questions:

1. Should robots look very little or very much like humans? Why?
2. Are there dangers in giving robots too much control over our lives?

Discussion Questions

1. Do you think it's important to have the latest technological gadgets? Why or why not?
   ▶ Would you consider yourself to be **tech-savvy**?

2. Do you think it is possible to be **computer illiterate** and still be able to function in today's society? Why or why not?

3. What do you think are some of the factors that make it easy or difficult for people to adapt to new technology? Why?

4. How often do you use social networks, blogging, or message services?
   ▶ What are some of the advantages and disadvantages of each?

5. How important do you think it is for older generations to adapt to new technology? Why?

6. If you could have some of the latest **cutting-edge** technology, which products would you choose?

7. Do you prefer to write by hand or to type? Why?

8. Does technology make us lazy?
   ▶ Is that a good thing or a bad thing?

---

computer literate *(idiom)*: able to use and understand computers well
cutting edge *(idiom)*: the most modern and advanced level of a thing or idea
tech savvy *(collocation)*: knowledgeable about technology

LESSON 2

>> WARM UP

What do you think life will be like…

…one year from today?
…ten years from today?
…a thousand years from today?

Objectives:
/ Discuss certainty about the future

A. Perhaps One Day

Less Certain (guessing) → **More Certain** (almost sure) → **Very Certain** (positive)

| I **might** be able to build a freeze ray. | I **could** build a freeze ray, if I... | I **should** be able to build a freeze ray. | I **will** build a freeze ray and take over the world. |

Degrees of Certainty about the Future

PART 1 • Based on the situation, make a guess about the certainty of the following:

Situation:

The class starts in 10 minutes. I wonder who is coming.

- Josie texted that she's on the way.
- Nancy never misses class.
- Andy comes about half the time.
- Carl is in China on business. Who will and who won't be here?

Situation:

Next week, Jim is taking a vacation.

- He doesn't like getting wet.
- He has a picture of a camel on his computer screen.
- He enjoys spicy food.
- He speaks **fluent** Mongolian. Where is Jim going on his next vacation?

Situation:

I wonder what Mom's cooking for dinner?

- She said that she went to the store to buy meat.
- Grandpa can't eat beef because of his heart condition.
- It's Jack's birthday and he loves meatloaf.
- There's a recipe that calls for ground turkey on the kitchen counter. What will Susan cook for dinner?

fluent *(adj.)*: smooth, clear, and accurate

PART 2

What is the certainty of these things happening in the next 10, 20, or 100 years?

Example:

Food Replicator

A: *We **won't be** able to design a machine that can make food in the next twenty years.*

B: *It **might be** possible if it worked like a printer. It **could** mix ingredients together.*

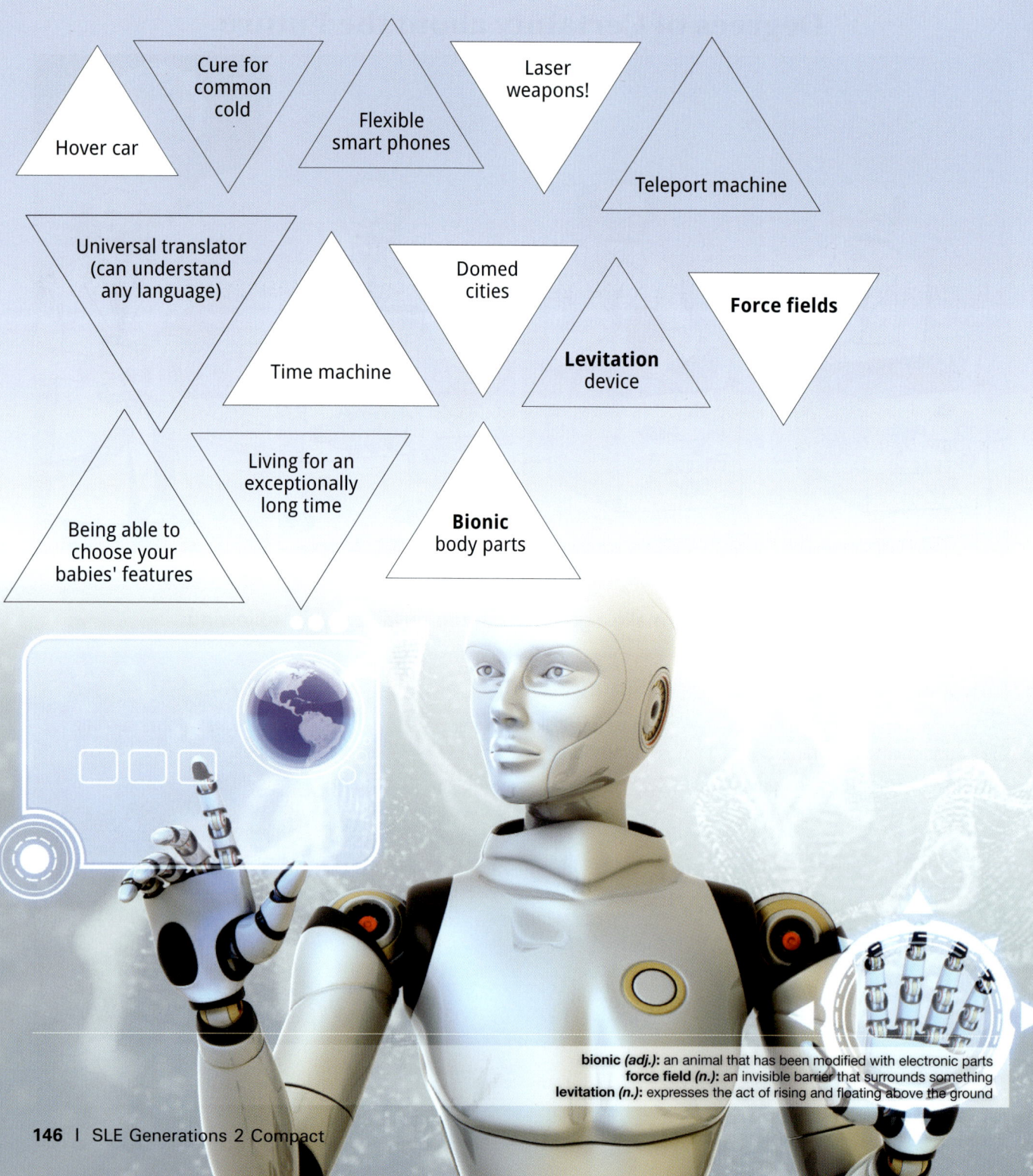

- Hover car
- Cure for common cold
- Flexible smart phones
- Laser weapons!
- Teleport machine
- Universal translator (can understand any language)
- Domed cities
- Force fields
- Time machine
- Levitation device
- Being able to choose your babies' features
- Living for an exceptionally long time
- Bionic body parts

bionic *(adj.)*: an animal that has been modified with electronic parts
force field *(n.)*: an invisible barrier that surrounds something
levitation *(n.)*: expresses the act of rising and floating above the ground

B. Time Keeps on Tickin'

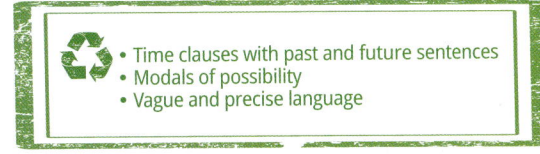
- Time clauses with past and future sentences
- Modals of possibility
- Vague and precise language

A. First pet
B. Learn to swim/ride a bike
C. Start school
D. First date
E. Graduate high school
F. First work experience
G. First trip with friends
H. Graduate university

I. Big trip abroad
J. Start career
K. Get married
L. Buy a house
M. Have a child
N. Become a grandparent
O. Retire
P. Other?

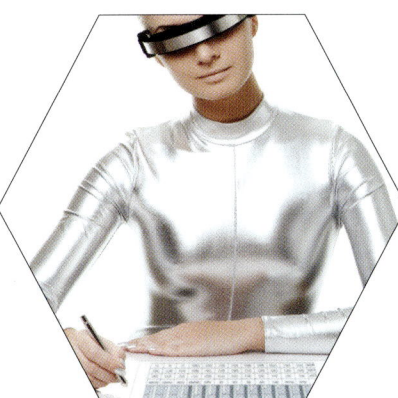

40yrs.   20yrs.   10yrs.   NOW   10yrs.   20yrs.   40yrs.

PART 1 ●

Place the important milestones that have already happened for you along the timeline above and compare them with others.

Example:

A: *I learned to swim before I started school.*

B: *Really? How old were you?*

A: *I was about four or five. How about you?*

C: *After I started school, I learned to swim.*

B: *Where did you go to school?*

PART 2 ●

Now make guesses about when the other milestones might happen in your life.

Example:

A: *I might go on a big trip abroad before I graduate university.*

B: *Where will you go?*

A: *I could go to Australia or New Zealand. What will you do?*

C: *I will buy a house after I get married.*

Do You Remember?

When comparing times in the future the verb that comes after time words like *after, before,* and *when* must be in the simple present.

Incorrect:
I will buy a house after I **will** get married.

Correct:
I will buy a house after I get married.

Unit 8 The Future is Now | 147

C. The Best Idea in History

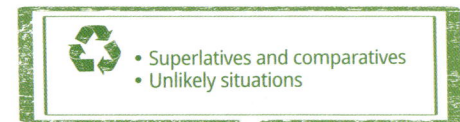
- Superlatives and comparatives
- Unlikely situations

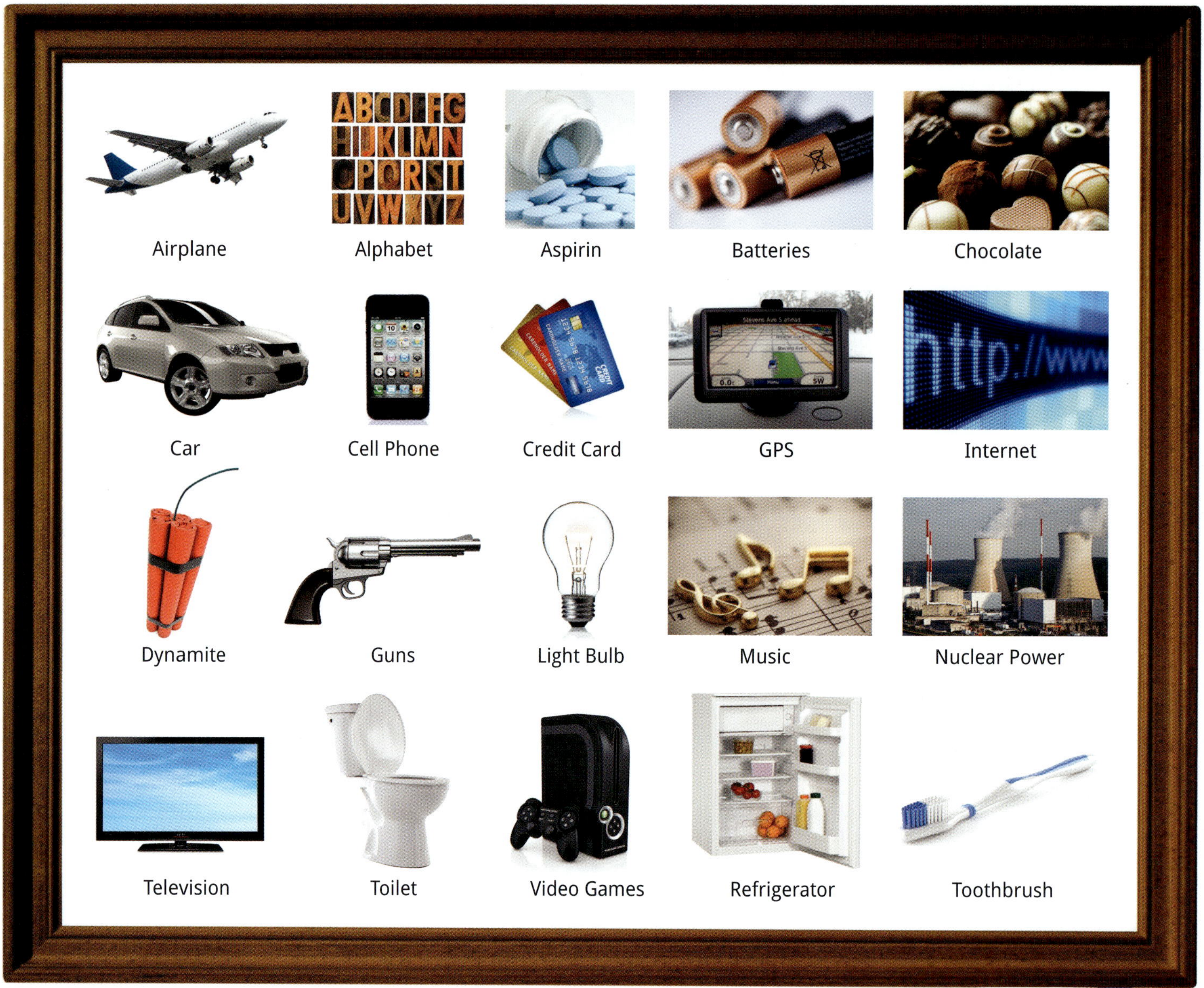

Airplane	Alphabet	Aspirin	Batteries	Chocolate
Car	Cell Phone	Credit Card	GPS	Internet
Dynamite	Guns	Light Bulb	Music	Nuclear Power
Television	Toilet	Video Games	Refrigerator	Toothbrush

PART 1 ● For each category, discuss which invention deserves the award for _____.

1. Most likely to cause health problems
2. Most useful when dealing with the opposite sex
3. Least valuable
4. Most damaging to social skills
5. Most helpful in an emergency
6. Most harmful to the environment
7. Most underappreciated
8. Most useful on a desert island
9. Invention that shouldn't have been invented
10. Most addictive
11. Most versatile
12. Most likely to disappear in the future

PART 2 ● How would the world be different without these inventions?
What would change?
What would you do if they didn't exist?

Discussion Questions

1. What are the pros and cons of owning a cell phone?
   - Do you think that cell phones ultimately improve people's lives?
   - Is it hard to **keep up** with the latest cell phone developments?

2. Would you rather communicate using only electronic communication devices (telephone, email, text message), or live with no form of electronic communication?

3. Which would you rather use for day-to-day transportation: a bicycle or a car?

4. What are some effects that **falling behind** can have on someone's life?
   - Do you know anyone who is **behind the times**? Is that person's life difficult because of it?

5. What types of technology are most important in modern society?
   - Can you think of any technology that's unnecessary?
   - What, in your opinion, is the greatest technological change of the past ten years? Why?

6. What future event are you most **looking forward to**?
   - When will this event happen?

7. What do you think I (your partner) will do tomorrow? Try to guess.

UNIT 8 REVIEW

How well can you use:
- ☐ Expressions about technology?
- ☐ Expressing future certainty?

What do you need to study more?

behind the times *(idiom)*: describes someone that is not following current trends
fall behind *(phrasal verb)*: to be unable to follow another's pace
keep up *(phrasal verb)*: to maintain the current level of something
look forward to *(phrasal verb)*: to anticipate something

Activity: The World Future Grant

Your city has received a $20,000,000 "World Future" grant to develop local infrastructure. The city government is now accepting proposals. Decide which changes to the list are most important, and develop a proposal to present to the mayor (your teacher).

Education:
- Provide scholarships to Engineering students in the city's most prestigious university: $6,000,000
- Develop a free computer-literacy program open to all of the city's residents: $6,000,000
- Provide a laptop for every student in local schools: $3,000,000

Sustainability:
- Install solar panels on major buildings throughout the city: $7,000,000
- Construct community gardens in neighborhoods throughout the city: $5,000,000
- Start a citywide recycling program that requires all businesses to recycle: $5,000,000
- Purchase hybrid cars for all of the city's emergency forces: $1,000,000

Health/wellness:
- Renovate the city's animal shelter to house a larger number of animals: $2,000,000
- Create a large public park in the downtown area: $1,000,000

Entertainment/Communication:
- Build a new shopping mall with cutting-edge technology to attract tourists from around the world: $7,000,000
- Install citywide free wifi: $1,000,000

Transportation:
- Build a new solar-powered sky train in the city's downtown area: $5,000,000
- Change the city's current public transportation system to improve safety features: $5,000,000
- Expand the public transportation system to reach new parts of the city: $5,000,000
- Widen roadways to reduce traffic congestion: $3,000,000

Mysterious Robot Creates Panic and Prosperity

By **Lawson D. Woods**, PNN

The local community is in an uproar over a mysterious robot that has been seen going from neighborhood to neighborhood causing chaos. While many think he could be dangerous, he is quickly becoming a hero to people he has met.

Several members of the community have had firsthand experience with the robot, whose body seems to be made of household appliances.

Angie Moss, a landlady for many apartments in the area, described her encounter. "That robot destroyed my bathroom wall! And then he did my hair. It's never looked better! Maybe I should ask him to do it again."

"I tried to stop him," says house owner Dave Davidson. "I hit him with a broom. He looked at me and asked, 'Just what do you think you're doing, Dave?' I told him I was trying to get him to leave my house, that's what!" When Davidson then attempted to force the robot to leave, the robot replied, "I'm sorry Dave, I'm afraid I can't do that. There is still a large wine stain on your wife's blouse."

Davidson's wife finished by saying, "Even though my living room has been destroyed, he did a really good job getting those pesky stains out!"

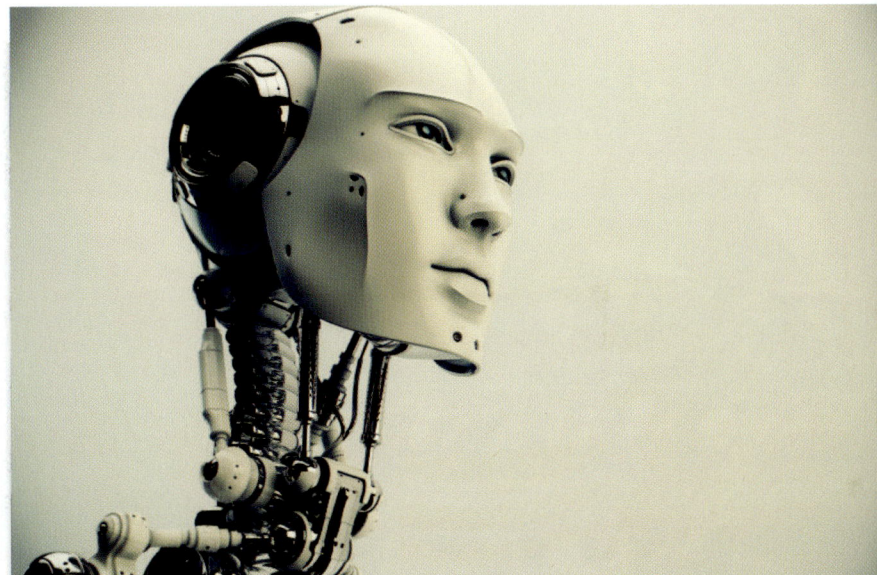

Another local, Cathy Clutz, came home from work to discover the robot cooking a twelve-course meal in her kitchen. "There were pots and pans everywhere!" exclaimed Clutz. "It was a mess!" Once the robot had finished preparing the dinner, he gently gave Clutz a back massage and tucked her into bed. "I have to admit, it was one of the most romantic evenings I've had in a long time. I told him he should call me sometime!" said Clutz.

No one knows where the mysterious robot came from, but we know where he will be going in the future. According to a MyFaceWorld advertisement, he will be performing at the New Motive Power Jazz Café this Thursday at 8pm.

A. Discussion
1. What kinds of things did the robot do to and for members of the community? Do you think the robot was more harmful or helpful? Why do you think so?
2. What are the pros and cons of having other people do things for you?
3. Do you think music created by technology (like computer software) should be considered the same as music created by people playing instruments?

B. Writing
Write at least a paragraph telling the story from the perspective of another person who met the robot. What damage did it do? Then, how did it help?

09
Shop Til You Drop
Shopping and Preferences

Objectives:
/ Describe products
/ Listen to a story about shopping for cell phones

WARM UP

1. Where is the best place to buy…
2. What is your favorite kind or brand of…

- Coffee?
- Cosmetics?
- Phones?
- Toys?
- Cars?
- Fashion accessories?
- Candy?
- Clothing?

IDIOMS

- **Window shopping**
  I don't have any money, so I can only go *window shopping*.
- **Corner the market**
  They were really able to *corner the market*. Nobody buys anything else.

PHRASAL VERBS

- **Pick out**
  My mom told me I can *pick out* a new jacket at the department store.
- **Buy into**
  I would never *buy into* the claims they make about their product.

COLLOCATIONS

- **Shopping spree**
  I went on a bit of a *shopping spree* last weekend, and now I'm broke.
- **Marketing strategy**
  Our *marketing strategy* is to target the youth market with celebrity endorsements.

Tongue Twister

Sarah saw a shot-silk sash shop
full of shot-silk sashes
as the sunshine shone
on the side of the shot-silk sash shop.

LESSON 1

A. Fashions Fade, Style is Eternal

Language Point: Describing Objects in Detail - Adjective Order

Determiner	Opinion	Size	Age	Shape	Color	Origin	Material	Noun
A	smelly		old		brown			boot
The		huge		baggy			wool	sweater
My	pretty					Japanese	silk	kimono
A pair of		snug	vintage					gloves

◇ Note: We rarely use more than three adjectives when describing an object.

PART 1 ● Take a peek into the family's closet and describe what you find.

> For each type of clothing, discuss what is and isn't fashionable.
> Choose one item from each section, and develop an outfit.
> Where could someone go in the outfit you chose?

PART 2 ●

1. What would you wear if you were planning on going...
   > shopping with friends?
   > to a job interview?
   > to a costume party?

2. Describe in full sentences what your partner is wearing using two to three adjectives before each item. Pay attention to the order of the adjectives.

baggy *(adj.)*: hanging loosely
snug *(adj.)*: fitting tightly

Unit 9 Shop Til You Drop | 155

B. London Calling

Pre-listening

1. How much did you pay for your cell phone?
   ▶ Do you think you got a good deal?
   ▶ How much is too much to pay for a cell phone?

2. What's the oldest thing you own?
   ▶ Did you pay for it yourself?
   ▶ How much did you pay for it?
   ▶ How often do you use it?

Listening TRACK 18-19

Grandpa Charles and Jack are shopping for cell phones. While listening, fill in the blanks with the prices of the different phones.

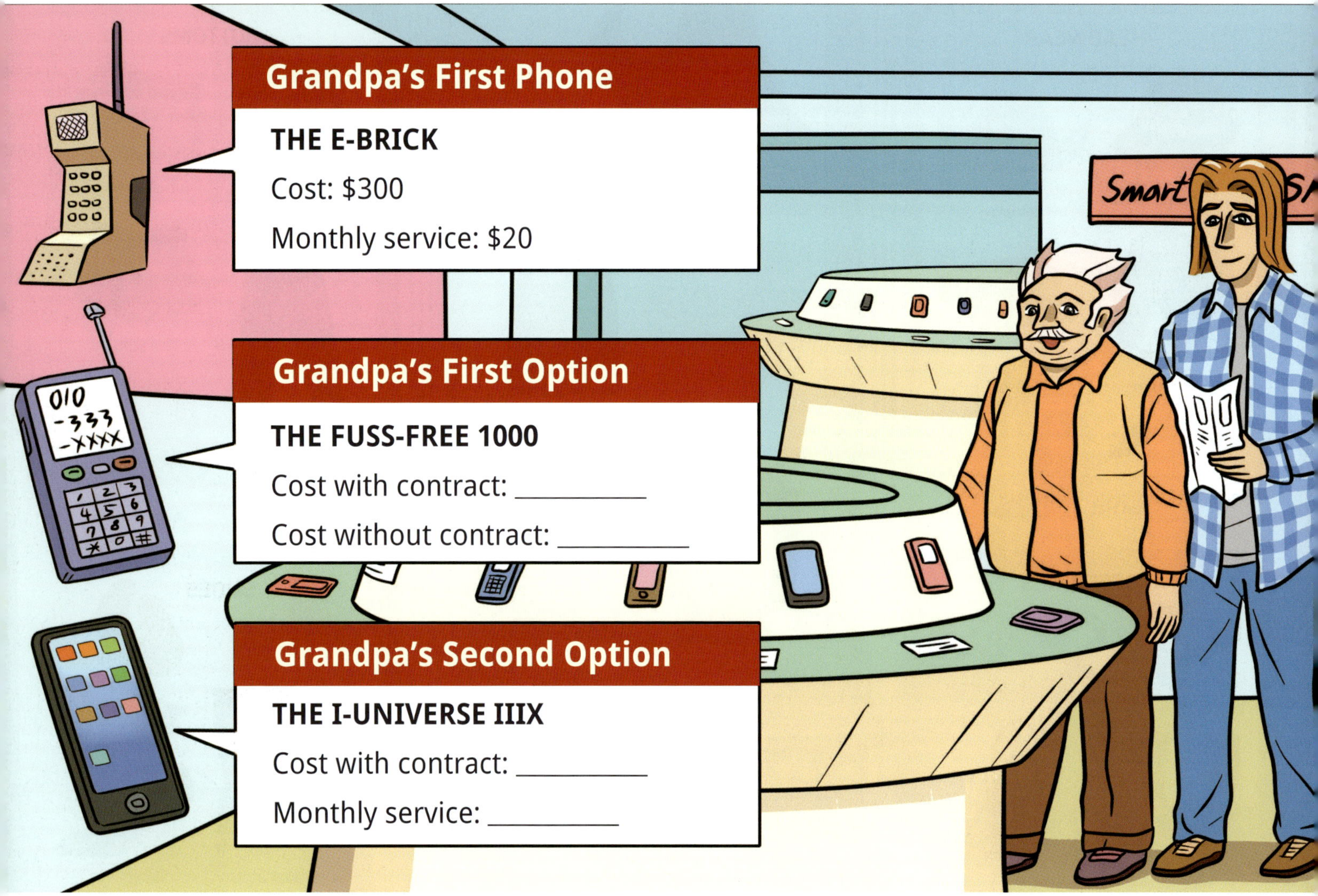

Grandpa's First Phone

THE E-BRICK

Cost: $300

Monthly service: $20

Grandpa's First Option

THE FUSS-FREE 1000

Cost with contract: _____

Cost without contract: _____

Grandpa's Second Option

THE I-UNIVERSE IIIX

Cost with contract: _____

Monthly service: _____

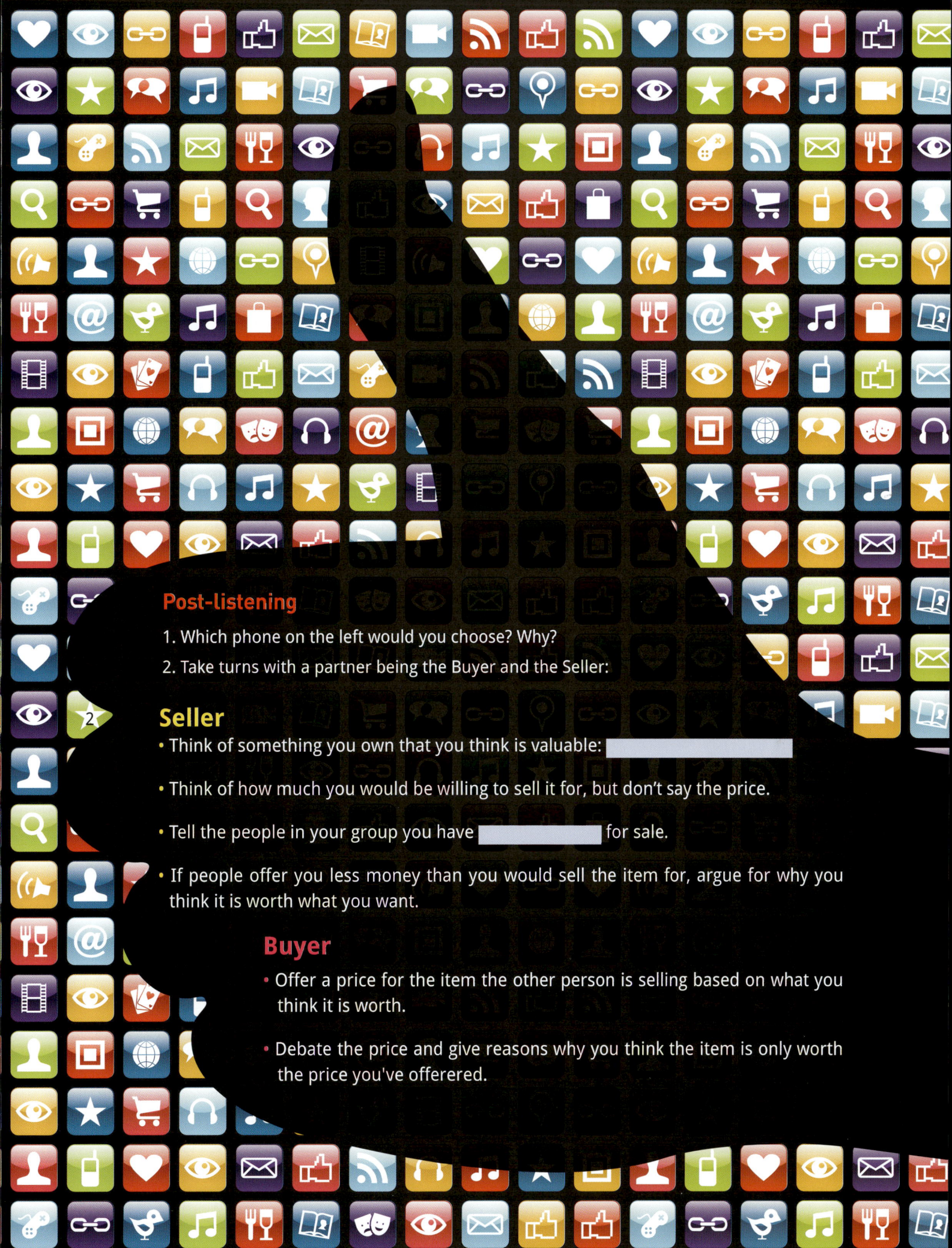

Post-listening

1. Which phone on the left would you choose? Why?
2. Take turns with a partner being the Buyer and the Seller:

Seller

- Think of something you own that you think is valuable: _____

- Think of how much you would be willing to sell it for, but don't say the price.

- Tell the people in your group you have _____ for sale.

- If people offer you less money than you would sell the item for, argue for why you think it is worth what you want.

Buyer

- Offer a price for the item the other person is selling based on what you think it is worth.

- Debate the price and give reasons why you think the item is only worth the price you've offerered.

C. Don't Count Your Chickens

Choose three investment suggestions from each situation below. Explain why you would choose each investment. You and your partner are…

> **Example:** A newlywed couple
> **A:** *I suggest we buy a new car because we need to plan for a family.*
> **B:** *Come on! I recommend we put that money into insurance policies to be safe.*

1. A newlywed couple

- House
- New car
- Future children's college education
- Jet skis
- Vacation condo
- Insurance (life, medical, and homeowner's insurance)

2. Co-owners of a trendy internet cafe

- State-of-the-art computer equipment
- Renovations (trendier interior design)
- Advertisement in the local newspaper
- Turn cafe into a chain and open locations worldwide
- State-of-the-art espresso machine

3. Recent graduates of a business administration program

- New cell phone
- Professional attire
- New car
- Downtown apartment
- Laptop computer
- Savings plan for graduate school

4. A recently retired couple

- Yacht
- Grandchildren's education
- Annual tropical vacations
- Convertible sports car
- Luxurious seaside condo
- Medical insurance

5. Co-founders of a small charity group

- Sponsoring poor children in Africa
- Helping local homeless people
- Sustainable farming in poor third world nations
- Bigger, more comfortable office with state-of-the-art equipment
- Hiring a celebrity as a spokesperson for the charity
- Advertising campaign to attract donors

6. CEO and Vice President of a large corporation

- Golf course
- Local charity groups
- Expanding into foreign markets
- Perks for high-level executives (golf trips, company cars, etc.)
- Employee salary increase and benefits package
- Employee team building activities to improve morale

attire *(n.):* clothing
morale *(n.):* level of confidence
perk *(n.):* additional benefit

Discussion Questions

1. What things are currently in fashion that you like?
    - ▶ What is currently out of fashion that you used to wear?
    - ▶ What fashion fad do you think should go out of style?

2. Is a person's fashion sense a good indicator of their personality?
    - ▶ Do people dress the way they feel?
    - ▶ What color or style do you think really **suits you?**

3. How important are name brand or designer clothes to you?
    - ▶ Are they worth the high prices?

4. What is your opinion of knock-off designer brands that are sold for a fraction of the price of the real thing?
    - ▶ Are you good at **picking out** the differences between a fake and a real item?

5. Have you ever been on a **shopping spree** or bought something impulsively and later regretted it?
    - ▶ What did you buy? Do you still have it?

6. In your opinion, which investments are safe? Why?
    - ▶ Which investments are dangerous?

7. Is it better to save money throughout your life or use money to enjoy your time? Why do you think so?
    - ▶ How should people create a balance between the two?

8. Aside from money, people also invest time. What are good investments of your time?

pick out *(phrasal verb)*: choose something
shopping spree *(n.)*: a shopping trip in which a lot of things are purchased
suit *(verb)*: to be the right thing for someone

LESSON 2

>> WARM UP

Objectives:
/ Expand descriptive skills
/ Discuss marketing strategies

Trendy or Tacky?
- What are your thoughts on the fashion styles below?
- What items would you wear?
- What would you never wear?

A. Information Overload

Language Point : Describing Feelings

When describing our feelings, we often use an adjective followed by a preposition and a noun or phrase. The preposition and noun/phrase show what caused the feeling.

▶ *I'm tired of companies that update their product every six months.*
▶ *I'm tired of shopping around.*
▶ *I'm tired of this old dress.*

◇ Note: Certain adjectives connect with certain prepositions. Just like learning when to use an infinitive or a gerund, these collocations can only be learned through practice.

PART 1 ● Ask and answer the questions about consumerism. Make an adjective + preposition combination using one of the prepositions from the list. Once you have used one preposition cross it off the list. Ask a follow-up question.

1 What are you worried *about* when shopping on the internet?
   ▶ *How often do you buy things on the Internet?*
2 Why is it important to be aware _____ all your options when making a big purchase?
   ▶ _____
3 How often are you satisfied _____ your purchases?
   ▶ _____
4 What's your favorite brand? What is the brand famous _____?
   ▶ _____
5 Are you ever amazed _____ the amounts of money people will spend on certain brands?
   ▶ _____
6 Have you ever been interested _____ starting your own business?
   ▶ _____

- By
- With
- ~~About~~
- In
- Of
- For

PART 2 ● Use an adjective + preposition combination in your answer and think of a reason why he might feel that way. How does Mr. Man feel about...

...his computer?

...the big sale?

...his new car?

...his cell phone bill?

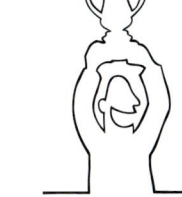
...his bowling skill?

| • Disappointed in | • Proud of | • Angry at | • Content with | • Shocked by |

B. Selling Ice to an Inuit

Look at the products below, and think of the best way to market them despite their **shortcomings**. Brainstorm every possible use for each product, then choose one product from each pair. How would you sell it?

Example:

Are you tired of wall decorations that don't do anything? Are you interested in singing animals?

If you answered yes, then the Singing Wall-Mounted Fish is the perfect product for you!

Use it to surprise and entertain your friends! Keep your cat company when you're out!

01 Singing **Wall-Mounted** Fish OR Bathtub with No Drain

02 Pile of Paperclips OR Old Rotary Phone

03 Unicycle OR Alligator Costume

04 Megaphone OR Santa Claus Monkey Toy

05 Bear OR Shopping Cart

06 Broken-down Classic Car OR Bird Bath

shortcoming *(n.)*: a failure or flaw

C. It Slices! It Dices!

You're a member of the Spit Polish Advertising & Marketing Company.

> Choose a product from below or make up your own.
> Develop a plan for how to market the product using the chart on the next page.

STEP 1 **Develop Your Product.**

    a. Who is your audience?

    b. What need does your product fill?

    c. How much will you sell your product for?

STEP 2 **Brainstorm Possible Advertisements.**

    a. Decide how you will advertise your product. TV Commercial? Radio spot? Website? Viral video?

    b. Are there any additional details you can add to improve your concept? A celebrity? A logo? A special promotion? A dance? A jingle?

STEP 3 **Develop Your Advertisement.**

STEP 4 **Present Your Advertisement.**

Example:

Product	Dazzler All Purpose Washing Liquid
Audience	Young to middle-aged people with busy lives
Need	Cleaning dishes, washing body, saving time, saving money
Price	$9.99
Advertising method	TV commercial
Additional	Celebrity endorsement and jingle

Advertising plan presentation: A commercial campaign with a catchy jingle performed by a famous celebrity. Because he has such a busy schedule, he doesn't always have time to wash his dishes. Now he can wash his dishes WHILE having his morning shower. Plates ready to go for breakfast! Jingle: "Hop in to freshen up, then scrub those dishes squeaky clean, every plate and cup!"

Your Product

Product	
Audience	
Need	
Price	
Advertising method	
Additional	

Sample Products or Companies:

Nozz-A-La Cola

Bent's Car Insurance

Mega Fit Health Club, Fitness Package

Sylvia's Skin Clinic, New Super Anti-Aging Skin Cream

Super Champ Dog Food

Hula's Dance Academy, Weekend Dance Camp

ReNewU, Stylist & Makeovers

All-Brite Toothpaste

Steve's Steak Bar, New Menu Item

jingle *(n.):* tune for advertising something
radio spot *(n.):* a radio advertisement
viral *(adj.):* message intended to be spread

Discussion Questions

1 What companies do the best job of marketing their brands?
- ▶ What do you like about their advertising?

2 How much of marketing is lying?
- ▶ How much do you **buy into** the claims companies make about their products?
- ▶ What specific examples can you think of where companies have exaggerated their product?

3 What company do you know of that has **cornered the market** on a product?
- ▶ Who do you think their marketing strategy is aimed at?
- ▶ Which demographic of people is the easiest to get to buy products?

4 What do you think about companies that aim their products toward children?
- ▶ What do you think of the way cigarette or alcohol companies market their products?
- ▶ Should the government be allowed to tell companies how they can market their products?

5 How do products that are from your country measure up in quality to those from abroad?
- ▶ What specific examples can you give of products from your country that are better?
- ▶ How about products that don't measure up?
- ▶ How can local products compete with foreign ones?

6 What do you know about guerilla marketing?
- ▶ Do you think this is a useful way to generate interest in a product?
- ▶ What marketing stunts have you seen in the past? Did it have an effect on you?

UNIT 9 REVIEW

How well can you use:
- ☐ Adjective order?
- ☐ Adjectives + prepositions when describing feelings?

What do you need to study more?

buy into *(phrasal verb)*: accept or believe something
corner the market *(idiom)*: to become so successful at selling a product that almost no one else sells it

Activity: The Perfect Gift

- Create a profile below, then share the profile with a partner. Your partner must come up with three possible gifts for the person you created and give reasons for their choices.
- Money and gift cards are not allowed.

Example:
A: *I need to buy a gift for a 35-year-old woman who is into sports.*
B: *What's the occasion, and how much do you have to spend?*
A: *It's for her birthday, and I only have about $4.00.*
B: *Uhhh. How about a…*

GENDER
☐ Male
☐ Female

AGE
☐ 0-2 years old
☐ 3-5 years old
☐ 6-12 years old
☐ 13-17 years old
☐ 18-24 years old
☐ 25-29 years old
☐ 30-39 years old
☐ 40-49 years old
☐ 50+ years old

HOBBIES/INTERESTS
☐ Food/cooking
☐ Sports
☐ Clothing/fashion
☐ Cosmetics
☐ Health
☐ Being outdoors
☐ Reading
☐ Television/movies
☐ Dance/music
☐ Painting
☐ Gaming
☐ Travel
☐ Other

OCCASION
☐ Birthday
☐ Anniversary
☐ Retirement
☐ Holiday
☐ Housewarming
☐ Other

BUDGET:
☐ Free - $5.00
☐ $6.00 - $20.00
☐ $21.00 - $50.00
☐ $51.00 - $100.00
☐ $101.00 - $500.00
☐ $501,000 - Money is no object

Segue

Ye Old App Shoppe
No-fuss apps for Grandparents

The Secretary — Free

Remember the days when you had an actual assistant who could actually figure things out for you? This app can't get you a cup of coffee, but it can do just about everything else on your phone. Just press the flashing red button and listen for, "You Called?"
Give a command, and get things done without having to put on your reading glasses.
"Call my son." No problem.
"Change the volume." No problem.
"Make that annoying buzz disappear." No problem.

Wha-cha-ma-call-it? — $1.99

"What on earth is this thingy for?"
"I can't for the life of me remember how to use this."
Ever been in this situation?
The Wha-cha-ma-call-it app allows you to take a picture of anything in your environment and send it to our dedicated team of whippersnappers. Get both an answer for what the thingy is and how to use it with simple step-by-step instructions. No need to interrupt your self-obsessed grandkids with what they think are obvious questions again!

Message Massager — $0.99

Are your grandkids texting you with ridiculous words that don't even make sense? With this handy app, you press and hold the text message in question and the question, "Massage?" pops up on the screen. Hit "yes" and instantly have the confusing message changed from this:
LOL Grams! B/F n I ROFL!
CUL8R , 143!
To this:
Laughing out loud Grandma! Boyfriend and I are rolling on the floor laughing. See you later. I love you!

A. Discussion

1. Which of the apps above sounds the most useful?
   • Which one do you think is the best value?
2. What apps do you use that you find really useful?
   • What do you like about them, and how often do you use them?
3. What do you think about products that are marketed towards a specific age group such as the elderly or children?
   • What examples can you think of that illustrate this?

B. Writing

Think of a new app that would be useful for a certain group of people, and write a short description of it that describes how it is useful.

10
The Art of Conversation
Communication Skills

Objectives:
/ Improve conversational flow
/ Listen to a story about a misunderstanding

WARM UP

Choose the best answer for each step, and say why you think it's the best choice. When starting a conversation with strangers, it's best to…

1 Approach…
   A. a large group of people.
   B. a couple of people.
   C. someone standing alone.

2 Start with…
   A. "There's a lot of people here today."
   B. "This is a really nice _____ ."
   C. "The weather today is really _____."

3 Talk about…
   A. yourself.
   B. what the person is wearing or holding.
   C. what the person does.

IDIOMS

- **Talk to a brick wall**
  A conversation with him is like *talking to a brick wall*.
- **Blow it out of proportion**
  She *blew the story a little out of proportion*. I wasn't that drunk, and there was only one clown.

PHRASAL VERBS

- **Strike up**
  I have a lot of difficulty *striking up* conversations with strangers.
- **Talk up**
  I think he spent a lot of time *talking up* the specifics to make himself sound better.

COLLOCATIONS

- **Take forever**
  This bus ride is *taking forever*! At this speed, we won't be there until next year.
- **Conversation piece**
  I love my new bag. It makes a great *conversation piece* whenever I go out.

Unit 10 The Art of Conversation | 169

LESSON 1

A. The Conversationalist

Language Point : Showing that You're Listening

We give quick responses or replies to something that another person has said to show the speaker that we are listening, and to keep the conversation flowing.

Personal Response

Showing Attention	- Right. - Sure. - Uh-huh.
Showing Interest	- That's interesting. - Is that right? - Oh, yeah?
Showing Surprise	- You're kidding! - Really? - I can't believe it!
Showing Sympathy	- That's too bad. - I'm sorry to hear that. - Oh, no!

A follow-up question can also be a personal response.

A: *I'm going to Hawaii!*
B: *You are? When?*

PART 1 ● Read the statement to your partner. Answer the statement with an appropriate response and a follow-up question. Try to keep the conversation going as long as you can.

> **Example:** My dog died last night.
> **A:** *My dog died last night.*
> **B:** *I'm sorry to hear that. How old was he?*

1. I won the lottery last night.
2. I broke my finger playing basketball.
3. My birthday is tomorrow.
4. I won't be here because I'm going on vacation.
5. My father was in an accident last night.
6. I really don't like this kind of weather.

PART 2 ● Make a statement about one of the topics on the right that is true for you. Read the statement out loud in a group. Every other member of the group must then reply and ask a follow-up question.

> **Example:** Most recent trip
> **A:** *I went on a trip to Kodiak Island.*
> **B:** *That's interesting. Where is that?*
> **A:** *It's off the coast of Alaska.*
> **C:** *You're kidding! Were there bears?*
> **A:** *Yes, everywhere. A bear chased me and I dropped my camera.*
> **B:** *Oh no! Were you really scared?*

- Most recent trip
- Favorite food
- Best class in school
- A really good movie
- Something sad
- An interesting fact
- An injury or illness
- Dream job

B. Conversation Breakdown

Language Point : Sentence Stress to Clear Up a Misunderstanding

Often in conversation, speakers will stress a particular word in a sentence. By placing stress on one word, you can tell someone that they have misunderstood you.

A: I want a **large** latte.   **B**: Oh right. You want a **large**, not a small latte.

A: I want a large **latte**.   **B**: Really? I thought you said Americano.

A: I want **a** large latte.   **B**: Okay. Just **one**, not two.

Pre-listening

Match the sentence below to the misunderstanding occurring in the picture.

1. Grandpa Charles: No sorry. I want a **large** pizza.
2. Grandpa Charles: I said I want a large **pizza**.
3. Grandpa Charles: I want **a** large pizza, please.

Listening TRACK 20-21

While listening, match each family member to their complaint.

1. Lisa
2. Martha
3. Richard

a. Wanted peppers
b. Trying to be a vegetarian
c. Thinks that a meat pizza is unhealthy

Post-listening

- Read the sentences below and choose one word in the sentence to stress.
- Clear up the misunderstanding by commenting on the stressed word.

Example:

A: *My friend bought a **new** sports car.*
B: *Oh I see. Your friend bought a **new**, not a **used**, car.*

- My friend bought a new sports car.
- How much are the red boots?
- When do you finish work on Friday?
- There are several pieces of cake left in the fridge.
- The best place to eat fish is near the beach.
- I don't hate the green knit scarf.

C. Finding an In

For each of the situations below, start a conversation to break the awkward silence. Decide who will break the ice. Choose a topic from below to begin the conversation. Use the question given or come up with your own.

Example: Sitting on a ski lift

A: *I like your boots. Are they comfortable?*
B: *Thanks. Yeah, they really are. I've been searching for boots that don't kill my feet.*
A: *Really? Me too. Where did you get them?*
B: *I bought them in a store called The Ski Barn in my hometown.*
A: *Oh yeah? Where are you from?*

Tip
A good way to start a conversation is to use a rhetorical question. A rhetorical question is a question that you already know the answer to.

A: *It's really cold here, isn't it?*
B: *Yeah! It's freezing. I should have brought a jacket.*
A: *Do you think the weather will get warmer?*

You are...

1. ...sharing a room in a London hostel with each other.
2. ...starting a job at a large company on the same day.
3. ....introduced by mutual friends at a costume party.
4. ...sitting next to each other on a long train ride to Beijing.
5. ...trapped in an elevator between the 19th and 20th floors.
6. ...standing in line at a tech convention.

Traveling
How long have you been here?

Friends
What's the best place to hang out around here?

TV/Movies
Have you seen the movie _____?

Shopping
Where did you buy your _____?

Family
Where are you from?

Technology
I see you have a _____. Do you like it?

Cars
What is the best car on the market these days?

Music
Have you heard the new _____ album?

Current Events
Have you heard about _____?

Work
What do you do?

School/Major
What did you study?

Past Experiences
Have you ever been to _____?

Hobbies
What do you like to do on your day off?

Sports
What do you think about the _____?

Discussion Questions

1 Have you ever been in a situation where you wanted to **strike up** a conversation but felt scared to do so?

- ▶ Where were you?
- ▶ What could you have done differently?

2 Do you ever have conversations with people sitting next to you on the bus or on an airplane?

- ▶ Do you enjoy these types of conversations, or do they make you feel uncomfortable?

3 Do you enjoy doing ice breakers at work or in classes, or would you rather simply get to work?

- ▶ What are the pros and cons of ice breakers?

4 Would you consider yourself to be a talkative person?

- ▶ When is it appropriate to talk a lot? When is it inappropriate?

5 Have you ever had a conversation with someone where it felt like you were **talking to a brick wall**?

LESSON 2

>> WARM UP

Objectives:
/ Use euphemism and exaggeration

Which of the questions below would you consider appropriate to discuss with a new acquaintance? Which are inappropriate?

Topic	Appropriate	Inappropriate
What do you think of the weather today?	☐	☐
Are you single?	☐	☐
How old are you?	☐	☐
What is/was your major in university?	☐	☐
What is your religion?	☐	☐
What's your biggest regret?	☐	☐
What is the scariest thing you've ever done?	☐	☐
What do you think about the president?	☐	☐
Where's the best place to hang out around here?	☐	☐

A. Chew Your Words

Language Point : Choosing Your Words

In conversation, speakers sometimes adjust their language to be more gentle or **harsh**.

Gentle
- *I think you might have a little spot on your shirt.*
- *Did you notice that you spilled something on your shirt?*
- *You have something all over your shirt.*
- *You have huge blue and orange spots all over your shirt!*

Harsh

PART 1 ● Brainstorm some gentle and harsh ways to say the following sentences.

1 "You have a piece of spinach between your teeth."
2 "You are a bad singer."
3 "I didn't like the restaurant."
4 "I never want to see you again."

> **Tip**
> A euphemism is a more delicate, indirect way to say something that would otherwise sound rude or harsh if stated directly.

PART 2 ● Look at the pictures below. Think of a gentle and a harsh way that you could mention each problem. Then, consider possible solutions to each problem.

Tom's bathroom is messy.

Norah is busy.

Jill is carrying too much stuff.

The boss is angry.

Kim looks upset.

The students' class is boring.

harsh (*adj.*): difficult to endure

B. A Little Bit Over the Top...

Language Point : Exaggeration

To exaggerate or **embellish** events or moments in a story to make it more interesting, use adjectives that express an extreme idea:

Okay → Good → Amazing   Not great → Bad → Horrible

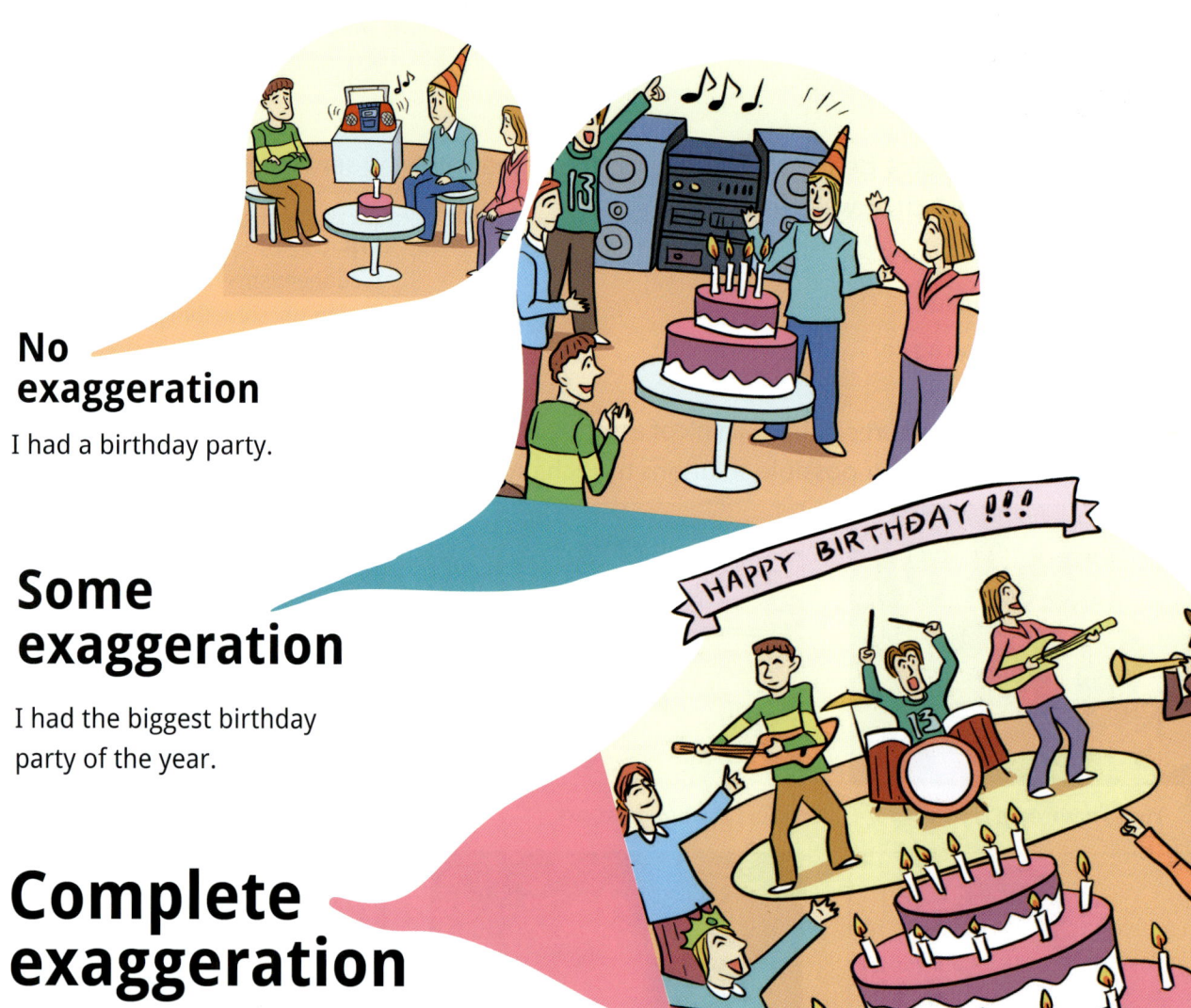

No exaggeration

I had a birthday party.

Some exaggeration

I had the biggest birthday party of the year.

Complete exaggeration

I had the biggest birthday party in the history of the world.

Embellish (v.): to make something sound better or worse than it is

PART 1

With a group…

- Ask the question.
- A second person must answer with an exaggerated statement.
- The next person should exaggerate even more.

Example: What did you eat for lunch?

A: *I had a hamburger.*

B: *Oh yeah? I had a huge sandwich.*

C: *I ate a lunch that was bigger than anything else I've eaten in my entire life.*

Questions:

- What did you eat for lunch?
- What did you buy the last time you went shopping?
- How often do you exercise?
- What sports do you enjoy?
- Have you ever seen a celebrity?
- What was the last trip you took?

PART 2

With a partner…

- Describe what you did last weekend. Give at least three details.
- Your partner(s) must restate what you said, but exaggerate everything.

Example:

A: *So, what did you do last Saturday?*

B: *Well…I didn't really do anything. I woke up late, watched a boring movie, and ate noodles.*

A: *She said she woke up so late that she almost won the world record for sleeping in. Then, she watched a movie that was so boring that it almost made her fall asleep again. After that, she ate an enormous bowl of noodles!*

Tip Lying vs. Exaggerating

It's easy to confuse a lie and an exaggeration. An exaggeration takes a true idea and makes it greater than it actually is for emphasis. Lying is giving a deliberately false statement with the purpose of deceiving others.

C. Exaggeration Evaluation

Tell a true story about yourself using the topics below. Exaggerate about one of the details. See if your partner can guess which one you are exaggerating about.

Example:

A: *Well, I went on my first date when I was really old. I was probably the oldest person on a first date, ever. The guy that I went on a date with was about the same age as me, so he was pretty old too. On the day of the date, the weather was terrible! It was so bad that we could barely even walk outside at all.*

B: *Wait! You're exaggerating about the weather, aren't you?*

A: *I was exaggerating about my age. I wasn't really that old when I went on my first date.*

1. **Your first date**
   - Your age
   - The other person's age
   - Where

3. **Something scary that happened to you**
   - When
   - Where
   - What happened

2. **A time you won/found something valuable**
   - When
   - What
   - Where
   - How

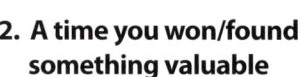

5. **A time when you were lost**
   - Who
   - Where
   - When
   - How
   - What happened

4. **A time when you won a competition**
   - When
   - Where
   - What kind of competition
   - How you won

6. **The number of countries you have visited**
   - What countries
   - When
   - How long
   - What activities

Discussion Questions

1 Have you ever been on a trip that felt like it **took forever**?
   ▶ How long was the trip really?

2 Do you think it is okay to exaggerate on your resume?
   ▶ What details do people usually embellish to make themselves look better?

3 Companies often exaggerate about their products and services in order to make more money. What do you think of this practice?
   ▶ Can you think of an example of a company or product that is advertised to be better than it is?

4 Do you think exaggeration makes a story more interesting, or do you prefer to hear the actual facts?
   ▶ Which shows can you think of that exaggerate stories to make them more appealing?

5 When couples fight, they tend to **blow things out of proportion**. Why do you think couples tend to make small things bigger than they actually are when fighting?

6 Have you ever had to talk up someone to make them sound better to….
   ▶ …your parents?   ▶ …your friends?   ▶ …your boss or coworkers?

7 Why do you think politicians use euphemisms in their language?

8 Can you think of a more euphemistic way to say…
   ▶ …war?   ▶ …fat?   ▶ …dead?   ▶ …handicapped?   ▶ …fired?   ▶ …ugly?

UNIT 10 REVIEW

How well can you use:
- ☐ Appropriate responses during conversation?
- ☐ Sentence stress?
- ☐ Euphemism and exaggeration?

What do you need to study more?

took forever (*idiom*): an extremely long time
blow it out of proportion (*idiom*): to overreact to something

BONUS BONUS

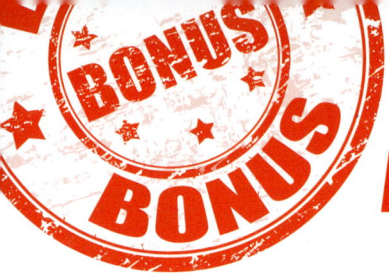

Activity : This is a...

1. The leader hands an object or a word to the left. (A pen for example)
2. The leader says, "This is a pen."
3. The person who receives the object must answer by saying, "A what?"
4. The leader replies again, "A pen."
5. The first receiver then passes the object to the next person, saying, "This is a pen."
6. The next receiver replies, "A what?"
7. The word is passed around the entire circle.
8. The leader then passes on another word to the right, following the same procedure.

Segue

Food online - Restaurant of the week

Popular Pizza People:
Just About The Best Pizza EVER!

Rating:

PNN food lovers will be thrilled to try the new pizza shop that just opened on Main Street: Popular Pizza People. The name is quite a tongue-twister, and the pizza puts a new "twist" on the usual pie.

I went to eat at this restaurant with my family. My wife and I got the "Veritable Veggie" pizza, which included a basil-tomato sauce and three kinds of cheese, along with mushrooms, spinach, onions, olives, peppers, and corn. All of the flavors of the veggies blended perfectly to make a delicious dinner, even without meat.

For the kids, we ordered a simple "Cheesy Tom", which had a basil tomato sauce topped with mozzarella cheese. The pizza wasn't greasy, and the kids finished their pie faster than my wife and I!

The restaurant had a trendy décor, but was very kid-friendly. In our opinion, the only downside was the price of the meal. For one medium and one small pizza, we paid about $35. Despite the prices, I highly recommend this for anyone who knows how to appreciate a good, original pie!

Comments:

 Lisa: I KNEW we should have ordered the veggie! My family just got a takeout pizza from Popular Pizza People last night. We had the Popular Pepperoni Pie—it was okay, but I would have loved to go meatless.

 Charles: Great review! However, I would recommend the Popular Pepperoni Pie. I picked one up for my family last night and everyone loved it!

 Lisa: Grandpa—is that you? I didn't know you used this site!

A. Discussion
1. According to the review, what are some of the pros and cons of Popular Pizza People? After reading the review, would you consider eating at a restaurant like this?
2. How often do you look for recommendations or reviews when deciding where to eat? What are some of your favorite resources for information about good restaurants?

B. Writing
Write a review of a restaurant where you've eaten. Describe the pros and cons of the restaurant, and write whether or not you recommend it to others.

11
Good Intentions
Success and Failure

Objectives:
/ Define concepts using gerunds
/ Listen to a story about a high school dance

WARM UP

Which of the following people best fits your idea of success? Why?

1 Allie: 40-year-old musical actress, married but has no time for kids
2 Aaron: 30-year-old adventurer, climbed most of the world's highest mountains, single, unemployed and lives in his parents' basement
3 Don: 45-year-old advertising executive, workaholic, divorced with two kids, rich
4 Margie: 35-year-old stay-at-home mother of three, happily married for ten years

IDIOMS

- **If all else fails**
  It's a big dream, but *if all else fails,* I can always go back to my old job.

- **Key to success**
  In marketing, understanding the customer is the *key to success.*

PHRASAL VERBS

- **Go under**
  It was terrible when their business *went under.* I felt really bad for the family.

- **Pull something off**
  It's going to be really tough to *pull this off,* but when we do, we'll be rich!

COLLOCATIONS

- **Measure success**
  I wouldn't *measure success* by how many degrees a person has. It's more about experience.

- **Without fail**
  Without fail, every time I go to Paris on vacation, it's raining.

TONGUE TWISTER

Theo Thistle is a successful thistle-sifter.
While sifting a sieve full of un-sifted thistles,
he thrust three thousand thistles through the thick of his thumb.

LESSON 1

A. The Ladder to Success

Language Point : Defining Concepts

Gerund phrases can be used to define abstract terms such as success.

Example:
A: *I think success is **having lots of close friends and family.***
B: *I would say that success is **making lots of money.***

PART 1
Choose 5 of the items below that represent your personal idea of success.

Success is...

- ...being married.
- ...living alone.
- ...being powerful.
- ...being independent.
- ...being healthy.
- ...having many friends.
- ...being in love.
- ...traveling wherever you want.
- ...being beautiful/handsome.
- ...speaking more than one language.
- ...having children.
- ...being on television.
- ...starting your own business.
- ...being able to purchase anything you want.
- ...having the freedom to _____.
- ...studying (subject) at (university).
- ...retiring early.
- ...saving lives.
- ...inventing something new.
- ...making other people happy.
- ...working for _____.
- ...other _____.

PART 2

Ask your partner or group for their thoughts on what the concepts below mean to them.

> **Example:**
> What do you think happiness is?
>
> **A:** *I think that happiness is feeling connected to the people around you.*
>
> **B:** *I disagree. Happiness is watching your enemies fail.*
>
> **A:** *Wow. You need help.*

What do you think …

01 … happiness is?
02 … failure is?
03 … beauty is?
04 … intelligence is?
05 … responsibility is?
06 … love is?
07 … freedom is?
08 … luck is?

Unit 11 Good Intentions

B. Cry If I Want To

 • Speculation

Pre-listening

How did you celebrate your high school graduation? Based on the picture, pick out all of the things that might be upsetting Susan.

Listening TRACK 22-23

What things do Susan and Richard decide are important? What things don't matter?

What matters…	What doesn't matter…

Post-listening

- What jobs do Richard and Susan want?
- What does Susan say that life isn't about?
- What does Richard say that life is about?
- Do you agree or disagree with them? Why?

What do you think matters in life? As a class, come up with a list of what matters and doesn't matter.

What matters…	What doesn't matter…

C. Growing Pains

• Speculation

Look at the profiles of Richard, Susan, and some of their high school classmates. Speculate on what each classmate might do in the future.
- What do you think their careers might be in the future?
- What interests and hobbies might they have in the future?
- What kind of goals and dreams might they have in the future?
- What might their relationships be like in the future?

Example:
I think that Stephanie might become a chef, but she could also become a veterinarian.

Richard:
Favorite class: Composition **Clubs & activities:** Choir, Junior Varsity swim team, Future MBAs Club **Social life:** Captain of the swim team ~ Voted "best writer" by his classmates **Future goal:** To be a doctor

Stephanie:
Favorite class: Biology **Clubs & activities:** Photography Club, Glee Club, Community Service Club **Social life:** Voted "funniest" by her classmates **Future goal:** Knows she wants some sort of job related to animals

Kyle
Favorite class: Discussion & Debate **Clubs & activities:** Varsity football team, Class Treasurer, Jazz Band **Social life:** Voted "most charismatic" by his classmates ~ Voted prom king **Future goal:** To be a professional musician

Susan:
Favorite class: Calculus **Clubs & activities:** Soccer team, Class President, Cooking Club **Social life:** Voted "most likely to succeed" by her classmates **Future goal:** To own her own restaurant

Stan:
Favorite class: Composition **Clubs & activities:** Marching band, Junior Varsity football team, Future MBAs Club **Social life:** Voted "most indecisive" by his classmates **Future goal:** No specific wishes

Paulette:
Favorite class: History **Clubs & activities:** Cooking Club, Swim Team, Chess Club **Social life:** Takes classes at a local college because she says she is bored with high school ~ Voted "most likely to take over the world" by her classmates **Future goal:** To be a lawyer

Relationships:
- Richard, Stan, and Kyle are best friends
- Stephanie, Susan, and Paulette are best friends
- Richard, Stan, Paulette, and Susan have known each other since elementary school
- Richard and Stephanie are dating
- Susan and Kyle are dating

Look at the profiles of Richard, Susan, and some of their high school classmates at their 25-year high school reunion.

- Which information here surprises you? Which information does not surprise you?
- What do you think could have happened to cause each person to reach the point they are at today?
- Which classmate seems the most successful? Which classmate seems the least successful? Explain your choice.

Example:
I'm surprised that Susan married Richard. She was Kyle's girlfriend in high school. I wonder if she and Kyle are still friends.

Stan:
Interests & Hobbies: Watching television, playing golf **Career Notes:** Vice President of a chain of fast food restaurants **Wishes:** No specific wishes

Stephanie:
Interests & Hobbies: Walking her pet dog with her family, church choir **Career Notes:** Veterinarian **Wishes:** To start her own greeting card company featuring photos of animals, to open her own veterinary clinic

Richard:
Interests & Hobbies: Cooking, reading newspapers **Career Notes:** Assistant Director of Marketing at a small company **Wishes:** To retire from his marketing job and become a freelance journalist

Susan:
Interests & Hobbies: Reading non-fiction books, watching movies **Career Notes:** Owns her own catering company **Wishes:** To open a café featuring her own homemade muffins and cookies

Paulette:
Interests & Hobbies: Swimming, baking **Career Notes:** Lawyer at a well-known law firm **Wishes:** To become a partner at her law firm

Kyle:
Interests & Hobbies: Playing saxophone in a jazz band, coaching his son's football team **Career Notes:** High school Civics teacher **Wishes:** To help his son go to college on a scholarship, to become mayor of his city

Relationships:
- Richard, Stan, and Kyle are still friends.
- Susan and Paulette are still friends. They have lost touch with Stephanie.
- Richard and Susan are married.

Discussion Questions

1 Does your definition of success match your parents' definition of success?
- ▶ In what ways don't your definitions match?

2 Have you ever had a reunion with your high school classmates?
- ▶ If so, how did it go?
- ▶ If not, would you like to have a reunion?

3 What do you feel has been your biggest accomplishment in your life so far?

4 Do you think that mistakes and failures can lead to later success, or are mistakes always bad?
- ▶ What have you learned from your failures?

5 Think of a time when you were successful at something. What was the situation?
- ▶ What was the **key to that success**?
- ▶ What part does luck play in success?

6 Have you been successful studying English? Why or why not?

7 Can you think of a company that has **gone under**?
- ▶ What do you think contributed to the company's failure?

8 How important is it to have a backup plan **if all else fails**? Why?

key to success *(idiom):* the way to become successful
go under *(phrasal verb):* to bankrupt a business
if all else fails *(idiom):* something you will do if your plans do not succeed

LESSON 2

>> WARM UP

Objectives:
/ Discuss life decisions and concepts of success

What do you think the symbols above mean in relation to being successful? Rank the four symbols from most important to least important based on what you think is necessary for success.

◇ Note: The three activities that follow may be done separately or combined into a game. The score from each activity continues into the next with a result at the end.

A. Build a You

- From the rows below, ask questions to a partner or group to make a character, or choose which areas best fit your own life. Be sure to ask them why they chose what they did.
- Based on the numbers listed for each option you choose, add up the points from each category and put the total into the box on the right.

$	🕐	👪	⭐

GENDER	♂ MALE	♀ FEMALE	🕐 TIME	$ MONEY	👪 FAMILY	⭐ FAME
EDUCATION *What kind of degree do you want? Why?*	None	**High School** 🕐 +1 $ +1	**Bachelors** $ +2	**Masters** $ +3 🕐 -1	**Doctorate** $ +3 🕐 -2 ⭐ +1	
	🕐 +2					
RELATIONSHIP *What are you looking for in a partner? Why?*	SINGLE 🕐 +2	**Boyfriend/Girlfriend** 🕐 +1 $ -1	**Married** 🕐 -1 $ +1	**Married** 👪 +2		
CHILDREN *How many children do you want? (Combine points for each child you choose) Why?*	None 🕐 +2	**Kristin** 🕐 -1 $ -1 👪 +1 *Writing, Singing*	**Lee** 🕐 -1 $ -1 👪 +1 *Making Things, Fighting Crime*	**Ian** 🕐 -1 $ -1 👪 +1 *Sports, Food*	**Stephen & Ruda** 🕐 -1 $ -1 👪 +1 *Fashion, Fighting*	
JOB *What kind of job do you want? Why?*	None 🕐 +2	**Part-time Worker** $ +1 🕐 -1	**Office Worker** $ +2 🕐 -2	**Manager** $ +3 🕐 -3	**Business Owner** $ +4 🕐 -5 ⭐ +2	

B. Life Choices

For each choice, discuss what you would do in the situation. Give a reason why you would choose yes or no.		💲	🕛	👪	⭐
	Enter Points from Activity A:				
1. You have a chance to make a large amount of money working in a small, secluded country. The contract is three years. *Will you go?*					
YES 💲 +3 👪 -2	NO 💲 -1 🕛 +1 👪 +1				
2. You have been contacted by the local orphanage. A new government bill will give additional financial support to adoptive families. *Do you adopt?*					
YES 👪 +1 💲 +1 🕛 -2	NO NO CHANGE				
3. You have the opportunity to run for a political office. *Do you run?*					
YES 💲 -2 ⭐ +2 *You had to spend a lot, but you are elected!*	NO 🕛 +2				
4. You've been asked to help out in a top secret government mission. (You can go only if you have two or fewer ⭐.) *Do you risk it?*					
YES 💲 +1 🕛 -1 *In return they can **pull some strings** and get you a promotion ONLY if you're an Office Worker.* (Office Worker 💲 +2)	NO NO CHANGE				

5. You have the opportunity to learn a new instrument. *Do you? What instrument? Why?*

| YES $ -1 ★ +1 🕐 -1 | NO 🕐 +1 |

6. Taking the bus is a pain. *Do you buy a new car?*

| YES $ -2 🕐 +1 | NO $ +2 |

7. You are invited on a Single's Cruise. (You can go only if you aren't married.) *Do you set sail?*

| YES 🕐 +1 $ -1
You meet a wonderful person.
BONUS: You can get married if you want! $ +1 👫 +2 | NO   NO CHANGE |

8. A week long training opportunity! (You can go only if you have a job.) *Do you say yes?*

| YES 🕐 -1 $ +1 | NO 🕐 +1 👫 +2 |

9. You are thinking about changing jobs and becoming a monk. *Is it time for some deep contemplation?*

| YES $ -3 👫 -2 🕐 +3 | NO 🕐 -2 |

10. You are offered a chance to be on a reality TV show. *Do you want 15 minutes of fame?*

| YES ★ +3 $ +1 🕐 -2
👫 -1 | NO 👫 +1 |

Unit 11 Good Intentions | 195

C. Good Intentions

As a group, flip a coin to move ahead (heads: one space, tails: two spaces). If you land on...
CHANCE: Each person chooses one of the numbers for themselves, then look on the next page.
SITUATION: Every person who answers gets the points.
CHOICE: Choose your own answer and explain why you made that choice.

START — With your whole life ahead of you...

01 CHOICE
You have figured out a way to cheat on your taxes. Do it?
- YES Flip a coin: Heads $ +3
- TAILS: You are caught, spend time in jail! 👪 -1 ⭐ +1
- NO $ -1

07 CHOICE
Your car breaks down
- Do you fix it yourself? 🕐 -2
- Do you pay someone to do it $ -2

06 SITUATION
Bad economy. You need to downsize your budget. What is something in your day-to-day life that you will give up to save money? Why?
$ +1

08 CHANCE
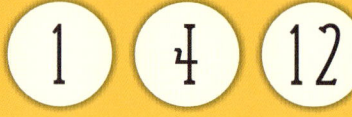
1   4   12

10 CHANCE

3   6   11

09 SITUATION
You want a little more time to relax. What is one thing you can cut out of your schedule to free up time? Why?
🕐 +1

196 | SLE Generations 2 Compact

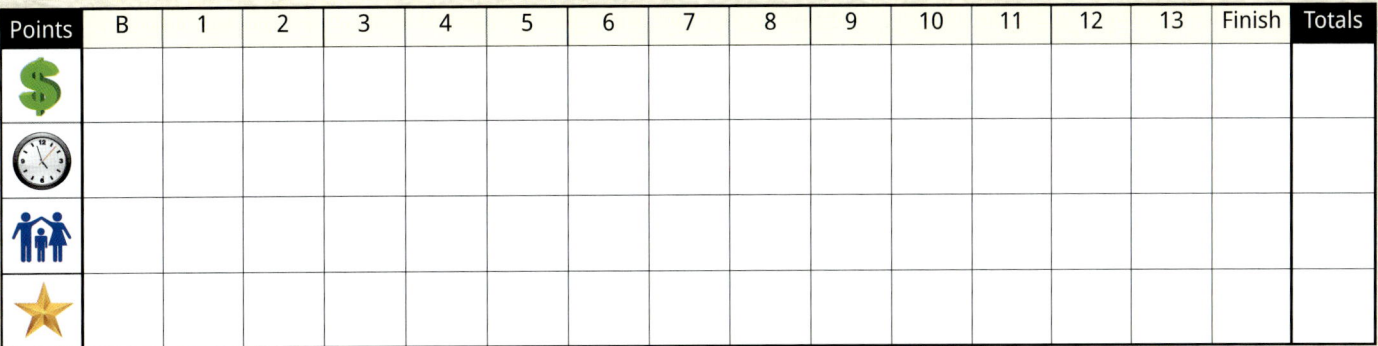

02 SITUATION
Your best friend has a child. Their child's report card was very bad. Give your friend advice.

👪 +1

03 CHOICE
Adopt a pet

YES 👪 +1 $ -1 🕐 -1

NO 🕐 +1

What kind of pet would you adopt?

04 SITUATION
You've started a blog. What is it about? Be specific.

⭐ +1

05 CHANCE
2   9   10

11 CHOICE
Your parents can no longer take care of themselves.

Do you take them in? 👪 +1 🕐 -1

Or put them in a home? $ -2 🕐 +1

12 CHANCE

13 FINAL DECISION
Do you ditch your career and become an actor, singer, painter, baseball player, etc? What do go for?

YES Flip a coin: Heads ⭐ +3 $ +2

TAILS: $ -2

NO 🕐 +1 👪 +1

FINISH
Do you want to retire early?

YES $ -3 🕐 +2

NO 🕐 -1 👪 -1 $ +2

CHANCE!

01 You published a book! *What was it about?* Now you have to sign lots of autographs.
🕐 -1   💲 +1   ⭐ +1

02 Demoted! Lose one level at your job. *What bad habit do you think got you demoted?*
💲 -1

03 Embarrassing situation. *What happened that made you so embarrassed?*
⭐ -1

04 News interview! You were interviewed on a major news network. *What was the interview about?*
⭐ +1

05 Sudden surgery! It's okay, you didn't need that organ anyway. You also get lots of bed rest! *What happened?*
🕐 +1   💲 -1

06 Uh-oh. Big unpaid debt. *What did you buy on credit?*
💲 -1

07 Oopsie, baby! Congrats on the new baby. *What do you name the little bundle of joy?*
🕐 -1   💲 -1   👪 +1

08 You won a national beauty contest! You're in high demand! *What shows are you going to appear on?*
⭐ +2   👪 -1

09 Promoted!
💲 +1 What's your new title?
If you are a "business owner":
💲 +2 for opening a new store. *What kind of business is it?*

10 Employee of the Month! *What good habit do you think got you the award?*
⭐ +1   💲 +1

11 Holy cow, you won the lotto! *What do you plan to do with the money?*
💲 +3

12 Someone robbed a bank, and they look just like you! *Did you do it?*
⭐ +1

Score Card

	Negative Points	1-4	5-10	11-15
💲	How's life under the bridge?	You manage to scrape by but you can't afford a lot of luxuries.	You live comfortably. You have what you need and much of what you wanted.	You have more money than you know what to do with!
🕐	You're so busy, it's unhealthy! Hope you have time to see a doctor!	You barely find time for yourself. You daydream of a vacation...	Your time management skills are excellent!	You're as free as a bird! You are the envy of your busy friends!
⭐	You don't even recognize yourself in the mirror.	You get a friendly nod from people in your neighborhood.	You sometimes notice people staring at you in public.	What's it like to be so famous? Can I have your autograph?
👪	...All by yourself, Apparently you wanna be, all by yourself...	You sometimes wish you had a little more support when times are tough.	You are surrounded by a loving and supportive family.	You might as well be the Mafia you have so much family.

Discussion Questions

1. Based on this lesson, what do you seem to value most in life: time, money, fame, or family?
   - ▶ Based on your results, would you like to change any of your values?

2. Who in your life do you view as a role model for successful living? Why?

3. How do you measure success?
   - ▶ What does success taste like?
   - ▶ Is success a journey or a destination?

4. What responsibilities does the government have in helping citizens to be more successful?
   - ▶ Do you think it's possible to teach someone to become successful?
   - ▶ Do you believe that people must work hard to become successful?

5. Who do you think is the most successful person in your country?
   - ▶ What part does luck play in success?
   - ▶ Does success make a person happy?

6. What is something you have tried to pull off, but didn't succeed?
   - ▶ Can you think of an example of a famous failure?
   - ▶ Do you think most people fail before they succeed?

7. What can you do now to be more successful in the future?
   - ▶ What is something that you do and without fail it is always a success?

UNIT 11 REVIEW

How well can you use:
☐ Gerunds to define concepts?

What do you need to study more?

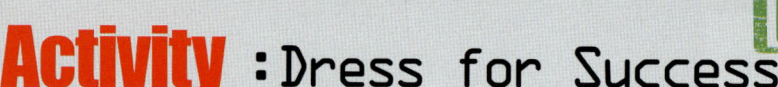

Adjective word order, making considerations, describing feelings

Activity: Dress for Success

Advise the people below on what to wear to succeed in each situation.

- What needs to be considered?
- Describe at least 5 things that each of the people below should wear.

Example: I'm going on a 20-km hike today, and it's supposed to rain the whole time! What should I wear?

You should consider what the terrain is like. You should also consider what the temperature is. If it's not too cold, wear shorts so that the legs of your pants won't get muddy…

Part 1

I didn't have time to shop for a costume, and I'm going to a costume party. I want my friends to be shocked by my costume. What can I put together quickly?

I am going on a date tonight at a fancy restaurant. I want to dress nicely, but I also want my date to be amazed by my unique style. What should I wear?

My friend is having a New Year's party. The invitation says to dress formally. I want my friend to be content with my outfit. What should I wear?

My friend is having a wedding at a beach that is famous for its hot weather. What could I wear that would look dressy but also allow me to enjoy walking on the beach?

I'm going to play tennis with the CEO of my company today. I want to look put-together, but not overdressed. What would be something that's appropriate for a tennis game?

I am worried about my interview for a job with a luxury brand. I can't afford their clothing, but I want to make a good impression! What should I wear?

I am going to a work event and the dress code is "smart casual". My boss will be angry at me if I look too casual, though. What should I wear?

Part 2

1. Have you ever worried about what to wear? Why were you worried? What did you decide to wear in the end?
2. Have you ever been horrified or amazed by an outfit? Why did you feel that way? Describe the outfit.
3. Can being fashionable make a person more or less successful?

Segue

The South Forsyth High School Reunion Society
Presents
Where Are They Now?

Stan Neville

An understated success story, Stan is the Vice President of the popular fast food chain, "McWendy King". His colleagues say that he is "exceptionally open-minded, and never tells a customer no!"

Married with seven children.

Paulette Martinez

Paulette made a name for herself by graduating top of her class from the prestigious law school of 'Cheatum U". She is currently an associate attorney at the firm of 'Bickers & Bickers'.

Unmarried.

Richard Thompson

Richard is climbing the corporate ladder. He is an assistant director of marketing at a mid-sized firm, where he has started a company-wide newspaper, "Know News, Good News". He and his wife, Susan, recently welcomed a new baby, Jane, into the world. Married with three children.

Susan (Carr) Thompson

What's that smell? It's the delicious smell of culinary success! Susan owns her own catering company (which has graciously agreed to cater this year's reunion) and has prepared meals for celebrities and politicians!

Married with three children.

Kyle Bartowski

Kyle is a high school history teacher. He coaches little league football for his son, Chase. He also plays in a jazz band, "The Bill the Robot Quintet". He invites you all to come down and hear them play!

Married with one child.

Stephanie Lee-Rickman

Stephanie has taken her love of animals to heart. A veterinarian for over ten years, Stephanie has recently started her own line of trendy greeting cards featuring cute, injured animals.

Married with no children.

Want to find out more about them and everybody else? Well, come on down to the SFHS Thirty Year Reunion! It'll be something to remember… at least until the next reunion!

A. Discussion
1. Which of the people above do you think is the most successful? Why?
2. Do you keep in touch with your friends from high school? Are you ever surprised by how much they've changed? Have any of them stayed the same?

B. Writing
Imagine that you will be attending a high school reunion soon. Consider what kinds of things you would want your former classmates to know about your life and accomplishments, then write a bio of yourself!

12
Make It Up As You Go
Storytelling and Inferences

Objectives:
/ Make inferences to fill in missing information
/ Listen to a story about a hike

WARM UP

A protagonist is the main character of a story. Brainstorm three famous protagonists:

1. _____
2. _____
3. _____

An antagonist is someone who opposes the protagonist. Brainstorm three famous antagonists:

1. _____
2. _____
3. _____

Who are the protagonists and antagonists in your favorite story?

IDIOMS

- **The story of my life**
  Every time I meet a nice guy, it turns out he has a girlfriend. It's *the story of my life*.
- **Truth is stranger than fiction**
  I didn't exaggerate the details at all. Sometimes *truth is stranger than fiction*.

PHRASAL VERBS

- **Make up**
  Did that really happen, or are you just *making it up*?
- **Plot out**
  We should sit down and *plot out* the details of the trip.

COLLOCATIONS

- **Take place**
  The movie *takes place* in a not so distant future where everyone speaks the same language.
- **Make a long story short**
  To *make a long story short* I forgot your present on the bus.

TONGUE TWISTER

Tell the tall tale of a tall tailed dog
That Tim told to tap a tall ale.

LESSON 1

A. Fables and Foibles

 Reported speech

PART 1
- Using the pictures below as a guide, tell the story with your partner. Include a description of the plot and what the characters say in each panel.

> **Example:**
> In the Grasshopper and the Ant, there's a lazy grasshopper that doesn't do any work. In Picutre A, the grasshopper asked the ants why they're spending all day working. The ant said...

- Discuss the **moral** of each story. How does the story teach the lessons listed? What other lessons does it teach?

> **Example:**
> I think that the moral of this story is that everyone should...

- Try to relate the moral to a personal story of your own or a situation where it could be applicable.

> **Example:**
> This reminds me of a time when...

1. The Grasshopper and the Ant

Possible lessons
responsibility, charity, **reap what you sow**

associate (*verb*): *to* mix socially
fable (*n.*): story that teaches a lesson
persistence (*n.*): the action of doing something without quitting
reap what you sow (*idiom/proverb*): everything that happens to you is a result of your own actions
subordinates (*n.*): those of lesser rank

204 | SLE Generations 2 Compact

2. The Tortoise and the Hare

Possible lessons

patience, **persistence**, pride leading to **arrogance**

3. The Boy Who Cried Wolf

Possible lessons

trust, lying, responsibility

4. The Lion and the Mouse

Possible lessons

pride, size doesn't matter, be nice to your **subordinates**

5. The Scorpion and the Frog

Possible lessons

human nature, the people you **associate** with, being **gullible**, learning to swim

PART 2 ● Now take one of the stories and retell it as a modern tale.

Example: *The Boy Who Cried Wolf* → *The Boy Who Texted Wolf*

Unit 12 Make It Up As You Go | 205

B. Reading Between the Lines

Language Point : Filling in Missing Information with Inferences

An inference is a guess about what happened in a story based on clues. These clues can be based on what the characters are saying or on your knowledge of the subject.

A: *He was so hot and thirsty. There was nothing but sand as far as he could see.*
B: *He must have been in the desert because it was so hot and there was a lot of sand and no water.*

Pre-listening

The pictures below tell two different stories. Decide whether the pictures belong to story A or story B depending on what you see. Make a guess as to where the story took place, who was there, and what happened.

Listening TRACK 24-25

Jack and Lisa are remembering a story of a trip they took when they were younger. Which story are they recounting? Listen for the details that happen between the pictures.

Banff National Park Story A

Saguaro National Monument Story B

Javelina *(n.):* a wild pig-like animal, also known as a peccary

Post-listening

Make up a story based on each series of pictures below. Where there is a blank box, fill in what you think happened.

Step 1 Choose a time and location where the story takes place, and give the character a name.

Example: *Last Thursday, Brenda went to the bank.*

#. 01

#. 02

#. 03

208 | SLE Generations 2 Compact

Step 2 Tell the story, giving as much detail as possible for each box. Ask information questions to move the story along.

Example: *Why did Brenda go to the bank? She went because she needed to take out a loan for a new house. What happened when she went inside?*

#. 04

#. 05

Unit 12 Make It Up As You Go | 209

C. The Black Out

 • Past speculation

You had a brilliant night. You think. You don't really remember. Look at the items below to piece together a story about what happened last night.

Example:
A: *Well, we might have gone to the beach.*
B: *I'm guessing because…*

- A pair of broken sunglasses
- A matchbook from the "Dance & Dine Club" downtown
- A receipt for twelve copies of the same cookbook 
- A fake flower bouquet with white ribbon
- A puffy jacket with sand in the pockets
- A text message: "When will we see you next? You left your umbrella!"
- Fish in the sink

Discussion Questions

1 What is the best method for telling a story? (Book, Movie, Game, Song, etc.)
  - Why do you think so?
  - In what setting do you like stories to take place?

2 What are some important lessons taught in the fables you heard as a child?
  - Do you think these lessons are still relevant in today's world?
  - Who told you stories when you were a child? What kind of stories did they tell you?

3 Do you think stories that are **made up** are more interesting, or do you prefer to hear true stories?
  - Can you give an example of the truth being stranger than fiction?

4 What kind of stories do you like to read?
  - What makes a story really interesting for you?
  - What makes a story really boring?

5 Who is your favorite literary figure (character)?
  - Why do you like this character?
  - If you could be a character in a well-known story, which story would it be?

6 Other than the protagonist and antagonist, what are some of the other types of characters in stories?

7 Should every story have a happy ending? Why or why not?
  - How do you like stories to end?
  - What's the best ending to a story you can remember?

make up (v.): to create

LESSON 2

>> WARM UP

Objectives:
/ Describe and develop characters
/ Practice telling stories

Give a short synopsis of a story or movie you like using the five plot points below.

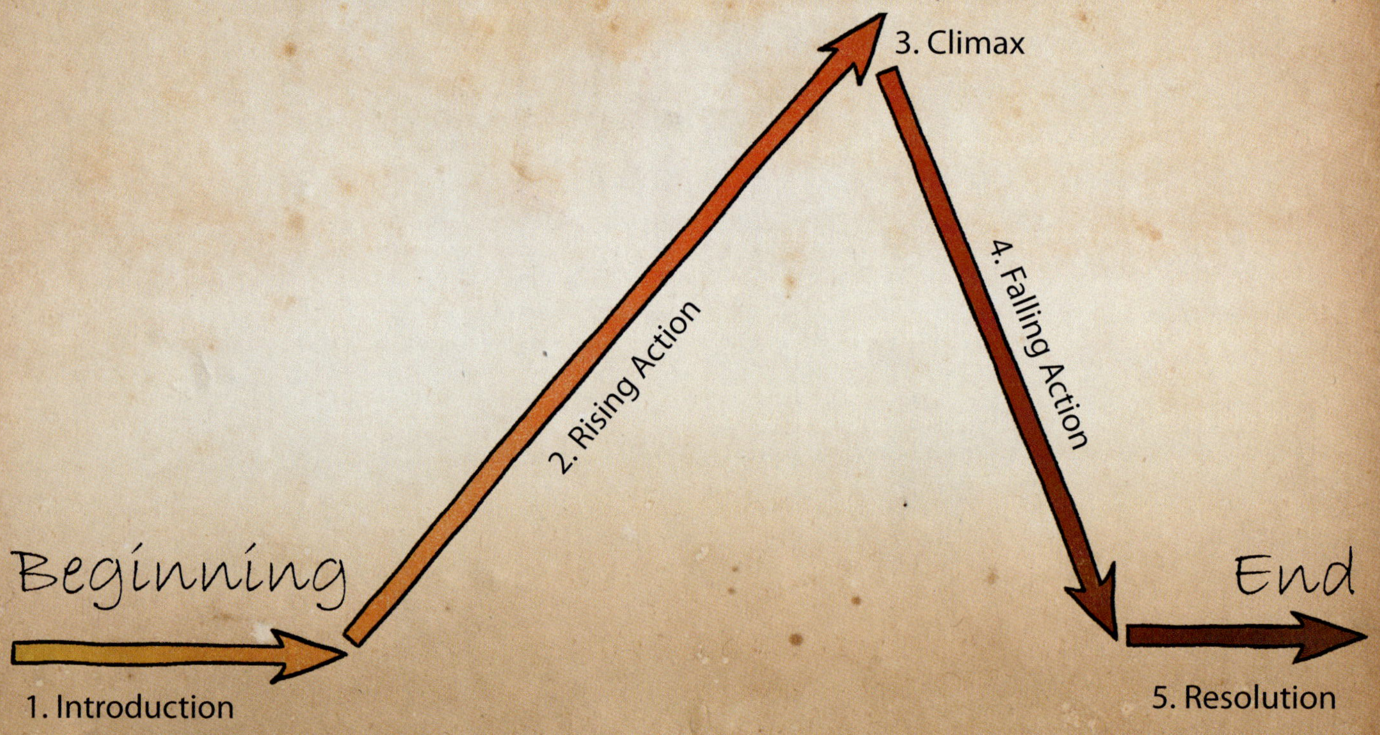

1. Introduction — Beginning
2. Rising Action
3. Climax
4. Falling Action
5. Resolution — End

A. Anecdotal Evidence

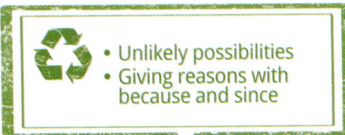
- Unlikely possibilities
- Giving reasons with because and since

PART 1
Choose a topic below that you would like to interview a classmate about. Think of five interview questions about the topic. As your classmate tells you about the topic, ask follow-up questions to learn as many details as possible.

> **Example**
> **A:** *Tell me about a bad date you've had.*
> **B:** *My first date was a really awkward experience!*
> **A:** *Oh no! Who did you go on the date with?*
> **B:** *I went on the date with Joe, a guy from my high school…*

Topics:
- A time when you helped someone
- An embarrassing moment
- A very happy or proud moment
- A very bad date
- A very sad moment
- A moment that changed your life

PART 2
Now that you've interviewed your classmate and learned a bit more about his or her personality, guess what your classmate might do, or how your classmate might feel, in each of the situations below. Give reasons for each guess. After sharing your guesses, discuss whether or not the guesses were correct.

> **Example**
> *If my partner Joe were invited to be on a reality TV show, I think that he would be the funniest person on the show because…*

Your partner…

…has been invited to be on a reality TV show.
  In this situation, your partner would…
  Your partner definitely would not…

… just found a stray dog on the street.
  In this situation, your partner would…
  Your partner definitely would not…

…has a 12-hour layover at the airport.
  In this situation, your partner would…
  Your partner definitely would not…

…was just pickpocketed on the subway.
  In this situation, your partner would…
  Your partner definitely would not…

B. Get Your Story Straight

Use the following pictures to create a story. You can use the pictures in any order you want. Make sure to use the appropriate verb forms.

C. A Storied Past

Work with a partner or in a group to create a chain story about two people. Use the past tense in the story.

Step 1 Write a profile for two characters.

A Name: _____	B Name: _____
Age: _____	Age: _____
Sex: _____ Occupation: _____	Sex: _____ Occupation: _____
Interests/Hobbies: _____	Interests/Hobbies: _____
Adjectives Describing Personality: _____	Adjectives Describing Personality: _____

Step 2 Choose the relationship of the characters from above.

Siblings	Lovers	Enemies	Old friends	Complete Strangers

Step 3 Choose a location.

In a train station	Near a famous landmark	On top of a mountain	Around the corner from:	On the other side of:

Chain story *(n.):* a story written collectively by a group of authors

Unit 12 Make It Up As You Go | 215

Step 4 Using the characters and setting chosen from the previous page, make a chain story. Choose a verb and begin the story. After using that verb, cross it off the list. Keep the story going by choosing another verb.

Alternate rule : **Link Four Verbs.** Begin with row 1 and choose a verb to start the story. This verb cannot be used again. As the opposing player, you may only choose a verb on the bottom row (row 1), or the verb on row 2 directly above the verb that has been used. Connect four verbs in a row to win!

Discussion Questions

1 Why do you think storytelling is an important part of our lives?
- ▶ Is it better to **plot out** a story before you tell it, or just make it up as you go?
- ▶ How much do people exaggerate when telling personal stories?

2 What are the qualities of a good story?
- ▶ What is the most important part of the story - the details or the conclusion?
- ▶ Is it better to **make a long story short** or be as detailed as possible?

3 What was the last thing that happened to you that's story-worthy?

4 Can you give a good **anecdote** of a time when you were…
- ▶ …late?   ▶ …lost?   ▶ …really hungry or full?   ▶ …scared?   ▶ …heartbroken?

5 What is lost when telling a story through technology? (messenger, email, etc.)
- ▶ What is the difference between having someone telling you a story and reading it?

6 What seems to happen to you all the time? In other words, what is the **story of your life**?

7 If your life were a story, what would the title be?
- ▶ Who would play you in the movie?
- ▶ How would you define the genre?

UNIT 12 REVIEW

How well can you use:
- ☐ Inferences to fill in missing information?
- ☐ English to tell a story?

What do you need to study more?

---

make a long story short *(collocation)*: to sum up a longer series of events
plot out *(phrasal verb)*: to make a detailed plan
anecdote *(n.)*: a short story about a specific moment or event
story of your life *(idiom)*: an expression for when something happens to you that has happened many times before

Activity: The Animal & the Animal

Develop Your Own Fable.

Step 1 Choose a lesson you want to teach. Ask questions about what problems exist in these topics.

Topic areas for lessons:

Health	Safety	Trust/Truth/Lying
Courage	Charity	Planning
Relationships	Work	Education

Step 2 Choose two animals that represent character types. Which adjectives describe the animals' personality?

Rat	Cow	Tiger	Rabbit
Dragon	Snake	Horse	Goat
Monkey	Chicken	Dog	Pig

Step 3 Make up a story with a conflict that teaches your lesson with the animals you chose.

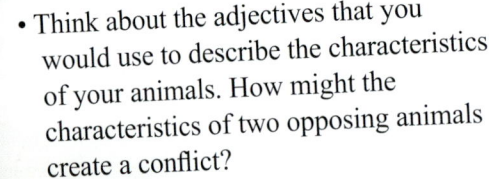

TIPS
- Think about the adjectives that you would use to describe the characteristics of your animals. How might the characteristics of two opposing animals create a conflict?
- In a typical fable one animal usually teaches the other animal a lesson that they don't see at the beginning.

Jack says:

Hey Danimal!! What's up?

Remember my sister, Lisa? We were just chatting about that awesome hike we went on a few years ago in Banff National Park. We still can't believe you scared off that angry moose!!

Keep in touch!

-Jack

Dan says:

Jack! What's up, dude?

Life has been good since that hike. I actually just got back from a trip in the Altai mountain range on the borders of Kazakhstan, China, Mongolia, and Russia. I ate some good food, met some amazing people, and saw lots of spectacular views (attaching a photo of one). I didn't even have to scare off any angry animals this time!

Got any hiking plans coming up?

-Dan

Jack says:

No hiking plans yet. I've been doing some work with an awesome band, The Crimson Kings. That's been keeping me pretty busy.

I checked out the photos you took on your trip. Looks like it was awesome!

-Jack

P.S. You should buddy Lisa, too! She wants to see the photos from your trip.

Dan says:

Will do! Glad you liked the pics. Keep in touch!

A. Discussion

1. Based on Dan's message and the photo that he sent, what are some inferences that you can make about his trip to Kazakhstan?
2. How often do you keep in touch with old friends and acquaintances via social networking sites? What are some other ways to keep in touch?

B. Writing

Find a photo from a trip you went on or event from your daily life. Write a caption describing the story behind the photo: where it was taken, why it was taken, who you were with, when you took the picture, etc.

Unit 12 Make It Up As You Go | 219

LISTENING DIALOGUES SLE Generations 2 Compact

UNIT 1 TRACK 2 and 3

Richard: *(office sounds)* Stupid printer. Hey, you! Can you help me?

Cheryl: Sure, what do you need?

Richard: I'm trying to get this printer to work.

Cheryl: Ah, I see. You have to push the pound key first.

Richard: Great, thanks! I really want to get this report in before five – I don't want to make a bad first impression on the boss.

Cheryl: That's probably a good idea.

Richard: Oh, hey, I'm Richard, by the way. Sorry. I should have introduced myself earlier, but I was in a rush.

Cheryl: It's not a problem. It's a pleasure meeting you, Richard. I'm Cheryl.

Richard: Hi Cheryl. So, how is the boss? I've heard that she is REALLY strict.

Cheryl: Oh, really? Yes, you could say that.

Richard: And that you don't want **to get on her bad side.**

Cheryl: Why not?

Richard: Well, I've heard that she can be a little…impatient.

Cheryl: Mm-hmm.

Richard: And I'd hate to get demoted, or even worse, fired, on my first day of work!

Cheryl: You're right. We wouldn't want that! But I'm sure if you show her you are considerate, hard-working, and organized, you will be just fine. See you later, Richard.

Richard: Thanks for the advice, Cheryl. Have a good day!

Cheryl: You too.

Jim: Hey Rick, what were you talking to Mrs. Stevenson about?

Richard: Mrs. Who?

Jim: Mrs. Stevenson. Our boss?

Richard: Wait…THAT was the boss? Oh no!

UNIT 2 TRACK 4 and 5

Martha: Charles, can you tell me what our **bank account number** is?

Charles: I can't remember what it is. Why do you want to know our bank account number?

Martha: I need to give it to this nice man on the Internet.

Charles: What?

Susan: Mom, what are you talking about? Please tell me who this "nice man" on the Internet is.

Martha: He's a man I saw on television who is trying to save the Egyptian Koalas. So I went to his web page and signed up. Now he sent me an email saying that I need to give him my bank account number.

Susan: Egyptian Koalas?

Martha: Yes, and I want to send him some money to help them.

Charles: Have you heard of koalas in Egypt before?

Martha: Well…no.

Charles: That's because there aren't any.

Martha: I was wondering if there were many koalas in Egypt…

Susan: No, mom, they're from Australia. I don't know who this guy is, but he is lying to you. It's a **scam**.

Martha: But he sounded so nice.

Susan: Sometimes people sound nice so they can **take advantage of** others.

Martha: That is so sad. Oh, well. Now what am I going to do with all of the money I am going to inherit from that wealthy Nigerian billionaire?

Susan: What?

Martha: I don't know how he got my email address, but apparently he wants to send me several million dollars. Such a nice man. I just need to send him $300 first…

Susan: Oh, Mom…

UNIT 3   TRACK 6 and 7

Lisa: So about our family vacation this summer…

Susan: Not this again, Lisa.

Lisa: I know you and Dad want to take a cruise but…

Susan: But what?

Lisa: Well…

Susan: Well?

Lisa: Jack and I really don't want to go on a cruise.

Susan: What? Why not? It will be a lot of fun!

Lisa: More like 'a lot of boring'.

Susan: Look, I've told you – there's a lot to do on the cruise ship.

Lisa: *(dryly)* You're stuck on a boat for two weeks.

Susan: If we upgrade our tickets, we can take fitness classes –

Lisa: boring.

Susan: Mini-golf –

Lisa: - which is more boring than fitness class.

Susan: Theatre shows –

Lisa: OR we can do something exciting!

Susan: Like what?

Lisa: I want to go skydiving!

Susan: Skydiving? Are you crazy? Can you imagine your father skydiving?

Lisa: Well, Jack thinks we should go camping in the mountains.

Susan: If we go camping, there might be bears! I am terrified of bears!

Lisa: Which is exactly why we should go skydiving.

Susan: *(sigh)* We're going on the cruise.

Lisa: There could be bears on the cruise…

Susan: Oh, hush.

UNIT 4 TRACK 8 and 9

Susan:

It was a dark night in the cold city. I had finished running errands after a long day of baking a very special strawberry cream cake. I came home around 8pm when I saw it. A terrible crime that had been committed. The cake. The cake I had spent the last two days making had been eaten. There were small pieces of strawberry and icing everywhere. On the table, the chairs, the floor. A single brown hair was found sticking out of the icing. My first clue. I immediately told everyone to come into the kitchen, the scene of the crime.

They all looked nervous.
My loyal husband, Richard; My sweet children, Lisa and Jack; My in-laws Charles and Martha. Nobody trusts their in-laws. And last, but not least, my dear cat, Mr. Squiggles.

The first question I asked them was the most obvious:
who had been home at the time of the crime. Everybody except Richard and Lisa. Richard was getting his hair cut, he claimed. Lisa had gone to the market.
Lisa also said she didn't like strawberry. My in-laws said they couldn't eat strawberry cake either. But then, nobody trusts their in-laws.
Finally, I walked around the room and noticed some of my "trustworthy" family members had icing on them. Maybe they just stepped in it. Perhaps it was evidence. Icing was on Jack's shoe, and there was more icing on Lisa's jacket. Mr. Squiggles had icing on his foot.
I decided to let them go for now. Jack had forgotten to do his chores, doing the laundry and feeding the cat. Lisa needed to do her homework. Richard went to the bedroom – he said he wasn't feeling well – and my in-laws went to watch TV. Mr. Squiggles stayed with me to think. Who to trust? It was a dark night in the cold city, and out there somewhere, the cake eater was waiting…

UNIT 5 TRACK 10 and 11

Richard: That was the water department on the phone.

Susan: Did they say we have to evacuate?

Richard: They said that we don't have to evacuate yet, but that we should prepare to leave if the water gets closer to the house.

Susan: Well we'd better start to pack the car in case we have to make an emergency exit.

Richard: Right. What are the most important things in the house?

Susan: Well, there's my family's quilt. I would hate not to be able to give that to Lisa.

Richard: Okay. I'll get my bowling trophy, those are hard to come by.

Susan: Oh, Richard. Couldn't you get the photo album instead? There's a picture in there of you with the trophy.

Richard: Fair enough. What about all the birth certificates, and diplomas, and……..

Susan: I've put all of those things in an envelope marked documents. It's in the drawer next to the…..

Richard: Computer! It's too big to bring. I'll back up everything onto a hard drive.

Susan: We have to bring the baby's special blanket.

Richard: And Jack should bring his guitar.

Susan: I could get the jewelry box.

Richard: We have to pack all of Mom's medication. We don't know how long we'll be gone.

Susan: It seems like we're forgetting something…………..What is it?

UNIT 6 TRACK 12 and 13

Lisa: What are you watching, Dad?

Richard: I haven't decided yet. Let's see what's on TV.

Richard: Oh, this show is great.

Lisa: I don't want to watch anything with people in suits….this looks way too boring. I'd rather watch something fun and exciting.

Richard: This is the Daily Gag Report, Lisa. This man might not look entertaining because of his clothes, but he's actually one of the funniest comedians on television!

Lisa: Let's change the channel. What about this show?

Richard: I don't know, Lisa. Don't you think that girl looks a little irresponsible?

Lisa: Why would you say that?

Richard: Because she's not wearing a seatbelt!

Lisa: This is my favorite show…it's called SoCal Life.

Richard: Let's keep looking.

Lisa: Oh! Stop there!!

Richard: Now Lisa, I don't want to watch this. That guy seems a bit young and rebellious for my taste.

Lisa: Dad, I know that this guy looks like that because of his tattoos, but you won't believe who he is!

Richard: Is he a criminal? Is this some kind of crime drama?

Lisa: No dad, this is James Block, the famous Smithson University engineer who just invented a new, ultra-safe car.

Richard: Wow…this looks interesting. Let's watch it!

UNIT 7 TRACK 14 and 15

Jack: Lisa, come here! Look at this!

Lisa: What is it?

Jack: You know how I made a website to help us find Mr. Squiggles a while back?

Lisa: Yeah. I wasn't sure if it would do any good. Any luck?

Jack: Actually, we have been getting posts from all over the world!

Lisa: What? How is that possible?

Jack: I don't know! Look at this one. This first picture was posted last week by a guy in Spain!

Lisa: You mean that picture of the beach?

Jack: Yeah. Ha, he looks so relaxed. Whoa, but look!

Lisa: Is that Mr. Squiggles with a…

Jack: …a lion! In Kenya! After Europe, he went to Africa!

Lisa: And there! A few days later. That picture with the elephant. He was in…Thailand! How did he get from Europe to Asia so quickly?

Jack: I don't know. But from there, he went hiking with some girl in Australia! It looks hot…

Lisa: No way! This next picture was posted by a group of scientists in…Antarctica?! Look at Mr. Squiggles! He's hanging out with a bunch of penguins! Can you believe it?

Jack: Next, there is Señora Camila in…Brazil? She said she had a dance lesson with a mysterious cat who looks a lot like Mr. Squiggles.

Lisa: How is he doing it?

Jack: I don't know, but maybe we'll find out soon. Look! This most recent post! A group of tourists in Hollywood, California took this picture! They must have thought he was famous!

Lisa: Really? He's already made it all the way around the world?

Jack: Yeah. Who knows, maybe he'll find his way home soon!

UNIT 8 TRACK 16 and 17

Susan: Hey, Dad. What are you up to?

Charles: Just putting the final touches on my robot, Bill. Say hello, Bill!

Bill: Hello, Bill.

Susan: Wow, that's really impressive. How did you do it?

Charles: Well, I used to be an engineer in my military days. Everything else I learned from the internet. I even bought the parts from a website. Next thing you know, I have Bill!

Bill: Hello, Bill.

Susan: What does it do?

Charles: Anything we want! With my remote control, I can tell Bill to do all kinds of things. Help with chores. Wash the cat. That kind of thing.

Susan: Really? That's incredible!

Charles: Yes, but…his main function is…

Susan: What, Dad?

Charles: It may sound a little silly, but I programmed him to play the trombone!

Susan: So now you have someone to play with! I think that's a great idea!

Charles: Let me show you how it…hey, where's my remote control?

Charles: Oh, Baby Jane, don't push that button!

Bill: Command accepted. Run, Bill. Run.

Susan: Oh my goodness! He just ran straight through the wall! Where is he going?

Charles: Bill? Bill, come back!

Susan: He's…it looks like he's gone, Dad.

Charles: This can't be good…

UNIT 9   TRACK 18 and 19

Charles: Thanks for coming cell phone shopping with me, Jack. It's been ten over ten years.

Jack: No problem grandpa. Your old phone looks pretty tired. It's definitely time for an upgrade.

Charles: I've only bought two cell phones in twenty years and I'm proud of that. It looks as if phones have become significantly cheaper. I paid over $300 for my first one back in 1992.

Jack: And because of inflation that phone would cost about $500 in today's prices.

Charles: That's true. Look at this one here. The Fuss-free 1000, it's free!

Jack: Well it's free if you sign a two-year contract. But you have to pay for monthly service for two years.

Charles: What's wrong with that?

Jack: Nothing really. The phone company gets their money back through how much they charge you every month. If you want to go that route Grandpa, I recommend this one. The I-universe IIIx. It has a touch screen, can surf the web, give you sports scores, and a whole lot more for only $299 with two-year contract.

Charles: But does it make calls?

Jack: Ha. Ha. Sure grandpa. You can even tell it who to call using just your voice!

Charles: And how much is that a month?

Jack: With voice and data it starts at about $70 dollars.

Charles: A month!? I pay twenty now.

Jack: Well, I think if you want to keep your current monthly plan, you could buy the first phone for $129 dollars without contract.

Charles: That sounds like a bargain.

UNIT 10   TRACK 20 and 21

Charles: Honey, I'm home!

Martha: perfect timing! Everyone is here, waiting on the pizza. What did you get?

Charles: Well, I couldn't remember exactly what everyone requested, so I just got a meat lover's special. It's got pepperoni, sausage, and bacon. Everyone likes meat.

Martha: Charles…I don't think that **everyone** likes meat…

Lisa: Oh yum, piz—wait, grandpa, I'm vegetarian!!

Charles: Lisa, I didn't think you were **really** a vegetarian…I thought that you were just being picky. You ate chicken at dinner last night, remember?

Lisa: Well, I'm **trying** to be a vegetarian….and meat pizza isn't helping me.

Richard: And I like **peppers** on the pizza, not pepperoni.

Martha: Charles, you should be eating **less** meat…this pizza really isn't good for your diet.

Charles: , okay. Maybe I didn't get everyone's absolute favorite pizza, but at least I **got** a pizza. If you'd like, I'll just take it over to the neighbors' house and eat it with them.

Richard: Well, we didn't say that we **won't** eat the pizza…

Martha: Yes, the pizza you got isn't **ideal**, but it's better than nothing.

Lisa: guess since the pizza is already here, I'll eat meat **tonight**.

Charles: That's what I thought…

UNIT 11 TRACK 22 and 23

Susan: (Crying) Oh! Umm…hi Richard. Sorry…

Richard: Ummm…Susan? I know that we don't really know each other that well, but…are you okay?

Susan: (Tries to make it seem as if she's not crying) Yes, of course. It's prom night!

Richard: I know…everyone says prom night is the best night ever.

Susan: Yeah…I just wish…(pause)

Richard: You wish…?

Susan: Well, this is going to sound silly, but I wish I could have been chosen as prom queen! I mean, Kyle's my boyfriend, and he's prom king…I should be queen, not Stephanie! I'm just so disappointed. Plus, I ripped my dress!

Richard: It doesn't matter…you look beautiful anyways.

Susan: That's sweet

Richard: Well, right now tonight seems like a huge disappointment, but I guess in the future it might just end up as another funny story.

Susan: Haha. Yeah…I guess life isn't about winning a crown at prom, right?

Richard: Right. I guess life is about appreciating what you have. 20 years from now, when I'm a successful journalist…

Susan: …and I own my own restaurant…

Richard: Right, and when you own your own restaurant…then we'll look back on this moment and laugh.

Susan: Yes we will…and being able to laugh at yourself is important.

Richard: So…do you want to go get some ice cream?

UNIT 12 TRACK 24 and 25

Jack: Hey Lisa. I was thinking about that family trip we took.

Lisa: You mean the one when we to see that famous national park?

Jack: . And it was sooo cold even though we expected it to be warm that time of year.

Lisa: Why were you thinking about that?

Jack: Well, I can't remember the name of the guy we met.

Lisa: We met a few people, Jack. Do you mean the guy who we went rafting with?

Jack: No, not that guy. The one we were hiking with when we got chased by that huge angry….

Lisa: Oh yeah! We called him Danimal because he shouted really loud and scared it off.

Jack: Uh-huh. And then we went fishing and made that amazing lunch.

Lisa: I remember that! He had lemons in his backpack! It was really delicious.

Jack: Yeah. That guy. I think he invited me to 'buddy' him on MyFaceWorld.

Lisa: Wow, really? What's he up to these days?

Jack: I'm not sure. Let's respond and find out.

GLOSSARY SLE Generations 2 Compact

A

Acquaintance *noun* person you know who is not a close friend — Unit 1
Adverse *adjective* negative, dangerous, harmful — Unit 8
An accident waiting to happen *idiom* an expression used to describe a situation that will most likely lead to a problem or accident — Unit 5
Arrogance *noun* behavior that shows you think you are better than others — Unit 12
Associate *verb* mix socially — Unit 12
Asteroid *noun* a rock that orbits around the sun — Unit 5
Attire *noun* clothing — Unit 9
Avalanche *noun* snow suddenly falling down the side of a mountain — Unit 5

B

Backtrack *verb* to return the same way you came — Unit 3
Baggy *adjective* hanging loosely — Unit 9
Beep *verb* to make a short sound as a signal — Unit 2
Behind the times *idiom* someone that is not following current trends — Unit 8
Better to be safe than sorry *idiom* the idea that one should always try to be careful
Bionic *adjective* having artificial or electronic parts
Blow it out of proportion *idiom* to overreact to something — Unit 10
Blunt *adjective* extremely straightforward with one's words and actions — Unit 5
Book (something) *verb* to make a reservation for a hotel, restaurant, etc. — Unit 3
Budget *noun* a plan for spending money — Unit 1
Burglar *noun* someone who enters a building illegally with the intent of stealing something — Unit 8
Buy into *phrasal verb* accept or believe something — Unit 9

C

Cannibal *noun* an animal that eats its own kind — Unit 3
Chain story *noun* a story written collectively by a group of authors — Unit 12
Chauffeuring *noun* personal driving service — Unit 4
Chew over *phrasal verb* to continue thinking about something after it is over — Unit 7
Compulsive *adjective* driven by strong drive to do certain things — Unit 5
Complaint *noun* a reason for not being satisfied — Unit 1
Computer literate *idiom* able to use and understand computers well — Unit 8
Consequence *noun* result — Unit 7
Conservationism *noun* the idea that protecting the environment is beneficial — Unit 5
Consumerism *noun* belief in the idea that acquiring goods is positive and beneficial — Unit 5
Conventional *adjective* normal, typical, or in accordance with custom/tradition — Unit 8
Conversation piece *idiom* something unusual that provokes conversation — Unit 10
Corner the market *idiom* to become so successful at selling a product that almost no one else sells it — Unit 9
Crack of dawn *idiom* very early in the morning — Unit 4
Creativity *noun* the ability to make new things — Unit 1
Cutting-edge *idiom* the most modern and advanced level of a thing or idea — Unit 8

D

Diagnose *verb* to determine the type of illness that someone has — Unit 8
Dedication *noun* committed to something — Unit 1
Degree *noun* document given to someone who has completed university — Unit 1
Demoted *verb* given a lower position at one's job — Unit 1
Disabled *adjective* a physical or mental condition that limits a person's ability — Unit 1
Dormant *adjective* not active — Unit 5
Drought *noun* a period of water shortage — Unit 5

E

Embellish *verb* to make something sound better or worse than it is — Unit 10
Engaged *adjective* promised to marry — Unit 1
Evacuate *verb* to remove someone from a dangerous situation — Unit 5
Errand *noun* small job to collect or deliver something — Unit 4

F

Fable *noun* story that teaches a lesson — Unit 12
Faculty *noun* the collective group of teachers at an educational institution — Unit 8
Fall behind *phrasal verb* to be unable to follow another's pace — Unit 8
Fashion sense *idiom* understanding of fashion trends — Unit 5
Figure out *phrasal verb* to make sense of, to resolve — Unit 6
Fired *verb* dismissed from one's job — Unit 1
First impression *idiom* the initial opinion of someone — Unit 6
Fix up *phrasal verb* to repair or improve — Unit 4
Fluent *adjective* smooth, clear, and accurate — Unit 8
Force field *noun* an invisible barrier that surrounds something — Unit 8

G

Get across *phrasal verb* to communicate or express information — Unit 6
Good judge of character *idiom* able to decide whether someone is good or bad easily — Unit 6
Go under *phrasal verb* to bankrupt a business — Unit 11
Grade point average (GPA) *noun* a number showing a student's average grade — Unit 1
Graduate *noun* a person who has earned a degree — Unit 1
Grouchy *adjective* having a bad temper or being in a bad mood — Unit 1
Guerilla marketing *noun* low cost means used for advertising — Unit 9
Guided tour *noun* a tour that is led by a tour guide — Unit 3

H

Handicapped *adjective* having a physical or mental medical condition that limits what someone can do — Unit 1
Hardworking *adjective* using a lot of time and energy to do something — Unit 1
Harsh *adjective* difficult to endure — Unit 10
Hiccups *noun* sound made that effects one's breathing — Unit 5
Hindsight *noun* the understanding gained after an incident has occurred — Unit 7
Honesty *noun* truthfulness — Unit 1

Horizon *noun* the line where the earth meets the sky — Unit 3
Humanoid *adjective* having the appearance or characteristics of a human — Unit 8

I

If all else fails *idiom* something you will do if your plans do not succeed — Unit 11
Intruder *noun* someone who enters without permission — Unit 8
Invisible *adjective* unable to be seen — Unit 3

J

Javelina *noun* a wild pig-like animal, also known as a peccary — Unit 12
Jingle *noun* tune for advertising something — Unit 9
Job security *noun* knowledge that an employee will not lose his or her job — Unit 1
Judgment *noun* decision making skill — Unit 1
Jump to conclusions *idiom* to make a quick decision — Unit 6

K

Keep up *phrasal verb* to maintain the current level of something — Unit 8
Keep your cool *idiom* to remain calm — Unit 5
Key to success *idiom* the way to become successful — Unit 11

L

Ladies' man *noun* a man who attracts women — Unit 5
Laid off *verb* dismissed from one's job due to economic reasons — Unit 1
Layover *noun* a period of time in which one is not traveling between two flights — Unit 3
Levitation *noun* expresses the act of rising and floating above the ground — Unit 8
Lifeboat *noun* a small boat that is kept on a larger boat in case of emergencies — Unit 7
Look back on (something) *phrasal verb* to think about the past — Unit 7
Look forward to *phrasal verb* to anticipate something — Unit 8

M

Make up *verb* to create
Make a long story short *collocation* to sum up a longer series of events
Measure up *phrasal verb* to be good enough — Unit 9
Mistake *verb* to accidentally think someone is another person — Unit 1
Misunderstanding *noun* Misunderstanding — Unit 2
Morale *noun* level of confidence — Unit 9
Mug *verb* to rob someone on the street — Unit 5

N

Narrow down *phrasal verb* to limit the amount of things being considered — Unit 4
Natural disaster *noun* a catastrophic event caused by forces of nature — Unit 5
Networking *noun* getting to know other people for employment or business purposes — Unit 2

O

Organization *noun* effective at arrangement — Unit 1
Outbreak *noun* the sudden spread of something such as sickness or conflict — Unit 5
Outdated *adjective* behind current trends — Unit 8
Overcome *verb* to deal with a difficult situation — Unit 1

P

Passion *noun* strong emotions about something — Unit 1
Patience *noun* ability to stay calm for a long period of time — Unit 1
Perk *noun* additional benefit — Unit 9
Persistence *noun* the action of doing something without quitting — Unit 12
Pick out *phrasal verb* choose something — Unit 9
Pick pocket *noun* a thief who steals by taking an item out of someone's pocket — Unit 5
Pick up (someone) *verb* to collect someone or something from a location — Unit 1
Play a trick *idiom* to trick someone into believing something as a joke — Unit 4
Play games *idiom* to try and gain advantage by being dishonest — Unit 2
Plot out *phrasal verb* to make a detailed plan
Poker face *idiom* a face that expresses no emotion — Unit 6
Prestigious *adjective* having a very good reputation — Unit 1
Promoted *verb* given a higher position at one's job — Unit 1
Proof *noun* something that shows that something else is true — Unit 2
Propose *verb* to make a suggestion — Unit 1
Pull something off *phrasal verb* succeed in doing something challenging — Unit 11

Q

Quit *verb* to stop working — Unit 1

R

Radio spot *noun* a radio advertisement — Unit 9
Raging *adjective* very strong force — Unit 3
Raining cats and dogs *idiom* raining very hard — Unit 3
Raise *noun* a higher salary — Unit 1
Reach out *phrasal verb* phrasal verb — Unit 5
Reap what you sow *idiom/proverb* everything that happens to you is a result of your own actions — Unit 12
Reference *noun* person who can give information about someone else's ability, etc. — Unit 1
Reliable *Reliable* someone or something that is there when you need it — Unit 6
Retire *verb to* end one's job or career because of old age — Unit 1
Run late *idiom* not coming at a scheduled time — Unit 4
Rush hour *noun* the busiest time for travel before and after work — Unit 3

S

Scam *verb* to trick someone into giving money	Unit 2
Scaredy cat *idiom* a person who is easily frightened or intimidated	Unit 5
Shopping spree *noun* a shopping trip in which a lot of things are purchased	Unit 9
Shortcoming *noun* a failure or flaw	Unit 9
Sidekick *noun* a hero's assistant	Unit 5
Sightseeing *verb* visiting places that are interesting when one is on vacation	Unit 3
Skeptical *adjective* having doubts about something	Unit 2
Skip school *idiom* to not go to school without permission	Unit 1
Sleep in *phrasal verb* sleep late in the m the day	Unit 4
Slip one's mind *idiom* to forget about something	Unit 7
Sober *adjective* not influenced by alcohol	Unit 1
Social skill *noun* ability to be friendly	Unit 1
Spark up *phrasal verb* to start a conversation	Unit 10
Speculate *verb* to make a guess about something	Unit 7
Snug *adjective* fitting tightly	Unit 9
Sunscreen *noun* that is put on skin to prevent sunburn	Unit 3
Sticking to a schedule *idiom* following a routine closely	Unit 4
Story of your life *idiom* an expression for when something happens to you that has happened many times before	
Strike up *phrasal verb* begin a conversation	Unit 10
Subordinates *noun* those of lesser rank	Unit 12
Suit *verb* to be the right thing for someone	Unit 9

T

Take a risk *idiom* to do something without knowing what the result will be	Unit 5
Take cover *collocation* to seek out a safe and protective place during a dangerous situation	Unit 5
Take forever *idiom* an extremely long time	
Take off *phrasal verb* to run away suddenly and quickly	Unit 5
Take over *phrasal verb* to assume power over something	Unit 5
Take precautions *collocation* to take steps to protect the safety of oneself	Unit 5
Talk to a brick wall *idiom* the person being spoken to does not listen	Unit 10
Talk up *phrasal verb* to praise something in hopes of making it popular	Unit 10
Tech-savvy *collocation* knowledgeable about technology	Unit 8
Tech support *noun* a service that helps customers with a product they have purchased	Unit 2
Therapist *noun* someone who specializes in particular form of treatment	Unit 8
Tornado *noun* air that moves over land and leaves destruction on the land that it touches	Unit 5
Trustworthy *adjective* someone or something that can be believed	Unit 2
Treat *verb* to deal with or care for an illness or injury	Unit 8

U

Undergraduate *noun* a university student who has not earned a degree yet	Unit 1
Upcoming *adjective* happening soon	Unit 1
Upgrade *verb* to improve	Unit 8

Viral *adjective* intended to be spread, or that spreads rapidly — Unit 9

Watch out *phrasal verb* to be alert for a problem or danger — Unit 5
Without fail *idiom* something always fails or happens — Unit 11
Witness *noun* a person who sees an action in progress — Unit 2
What's done is done *idiom* once something has been done, it cannot be changed — Unit 6

Use the following activities to review and expand upon what you've learned in SLE Level 2!

These Are My People

PART 1 • You have been chosen as the next Great Leaders of one of the following societies. Choose one or make your own.

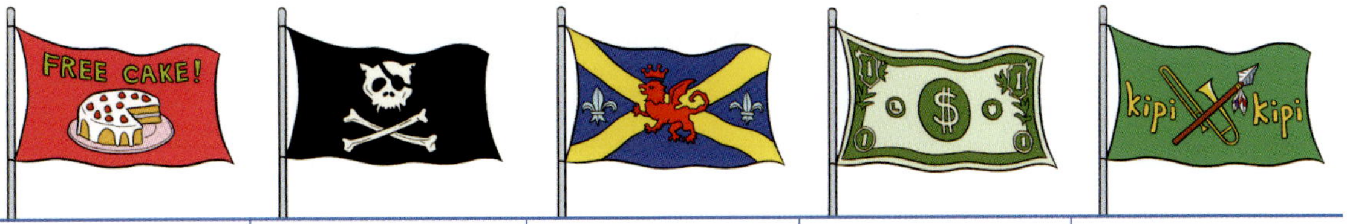

Nation	Free Cake	Squigglosia	Humberg	Costa Lotsa	KipiKipi
Motto	"Let Us Eat Cake!"	"Pet Me, Feed Me!"	"Tradition!"	"Show Me the Money!"	"KIPI KIPI!"
Leader Type	President	Lord	King or Queen	CEO	Prime Minister
Population	200,000	650,000	8,100,000	3,300,000	70,000
Biggest Export	 Food	Natural Resources	Labor	Technology	Entertainment
Land Type	 Plains	Forests and Series of Islands	Mountains and Deserts	Snowy Plains and Mountains	Jungles
Biggest Problem	Obesity	Large divide between rich and poor	Overpopulation	Pollution	Natural Disasters

Your Nation

Motto	
Leader Type	
Population	
Biggest Export	
Land Type	
Biggest Problem	

PART 2

As leaders of your new nations, you must decide on some of the customs of your people. You have been asked to pass a series of laws. With your partner(s), decide which of the three options you will choose for your nation.

Greetings	Shake hands	Bow	Kiss and hug
Fashion	All citizens wear a uniform that displays their social status.	People are free to wear any clothing they desire.	Everyone wears the exact same outfit to avoid **discrimination.**
Food	All food is a tasteless paste with all necessary nutrients.	Eating is a social experience. Tasty food that potentially leads to obesity and other health problems is common.	Everyone is required to grow their own food.
Education	Very strict educational system. Students are required to go to school for at least 15 years.	Educational system in which students are able to learn for themselves	Children do not attend school; instead they learn by working as interns from a young age.
Work	Jobs are assigned by the government.	There is freedom to do any job, but the society is highly competitive.	Every year, people are given a new job.
Money	There is no money. The government gives out necessities.	There is a free market system.	There is a **barter** system where all items are traded for items or services of equal value.
Entertainment	Every individual should be a part of the nation's entertainment industry for at least 15 minutes of their life.	Entertainment is made only with government approval so nothing offensive is presented.	There is no entertainment as it corrupts those who use it.
Social structure	Challenge authority to strengthen society.	Obey authority to strengthen society.	Most major decisions are made by a supercomputer.

discrimination *(n.)*: unfair treatment of a person or group
barter *(v.)*: to exchange services or goods without using money

My People Part 2: Cultural Perspective

Argue for or against each opinion – the symbol of your nation determines which side of the argument you must take.

FOR   AGAINST

 Internet and television should be censored by the government.

 Children should be raised by the entire community so everyone is responsible.

 Food and dietary concerns should be strictly dictated by the government to prevent health problems or obesity.

 The old and sick should be separated from the young and healthy in order to strengthen society.

 Every man and woman should serve in the military before being allowed to use any service paid for by tax dollars.

 Very attractive people should be forced to get ugly tattoos. Unattractive people should be forced to get makeovers.

censor *(v.):* to restrict in order to prevent threats to security/authority

My People Part 3: Model UN

The Five Nations

	Free Cake	Squigglosia	Humberg	Costa Lotsa	KipiKipi
Have	Food	Natural Resources	Labor	Money	Entertainment
Need	Entertainment	Money	Food	Labor	Natural Resources

Now that you've discussed the dos and don'ts for your society (as well as their world view based on Activity B) you must resolve the following issues in cooperation with the other societies. For each situation ask the following questions:

- What should we do?
- What could we have done to avoid the problem?
- How can your country help?

Example:
Many people from Humberg are trying to immigrate to its neighbor Squigglosia

A: *They could send the people to Costa Lotsa in exchange for technology.*

B: *Humberg should have trained them as singers. Then they could trade with Free Cake for food.*

1. There was a drought in Free Cake. Because of this, all nations are suffering a food shortage.

2. There is a conflict between KipiKipi and Squigglosia. Squigglosia refuses to give needed resources to KipiKipi because the news media of KipiKipi said some very bad things about the government of Squigglosia.

3. There was an earthquake in Humberg. Thousands are in need of aid. Based on your nation's exports, what specific aid can you send to help?
   ▶ If you are Humberg, what do you need? How can you help your people?

4. There will be an international sports competition in which all nations will compete. Everyone wants to hold the event.

5. A group of hackers in Costa Lotsa revealed that the Great Leaders of each nation are making a huge amount of money. People have started protesting all over the world because they think it is unfair.

6. Scientists from every nation are seeing an increase in global warming.

 **Bonus** Work together to discuss solutions to each nation's biggest problems mentioned in Activity A.

Literal Idioms

Match the idiom on the left to its literal meaning on the right. Then, discuss what you think the actual meaning of the idiom is and a situation in which you would use it.

Idiom

1. Break a leg
2. Pulling my leg
3. Frog in your throat
4. Crying over spilled milk
5. Thinking outside the box
6. My foot fell asleep
7. Butterflies in your stomach
8. Get out of my face

Literal

The Silver Screen   (Now in )

PART 1 ● Look at the movie posters below. What is the main genre for each? What are the subgenres?

For each poster below, make up a **synopsis** for the movie.
Include:
> How do the main characters meet or know each other?
> What is the primary conflict?
> What is the climax?
> How is the plot resolved? What is the final scene?
  Bonus: What would the sequel be?

Rated: G

Rated: R

Climax (n.): the most important or exciting point
Plot (n.): sequence of events in a novel, play, or movie
Sequel (n.): continuation of a story
Synopsis (n.): a summary of the plot

Rated: PG-13

Rated: R

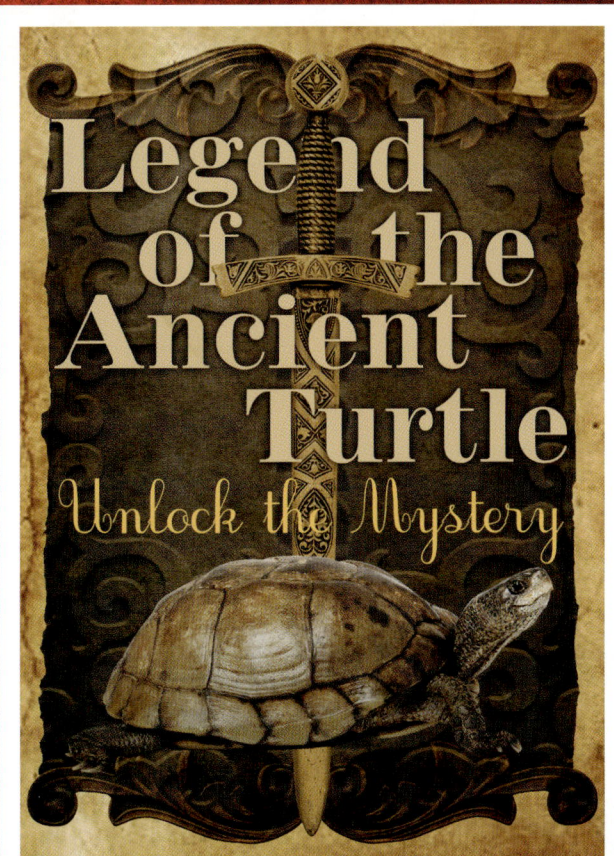

Rated: PG

Rated: PG-13

PART 2 ● Create Your Own Film

1. In a group, develop a movie of your own.
   Your movie needs:
   Title // Genre and Subgenres // **Cast** // Location // Plot // Tag Line
   If you need ideas, you can either make a sequel to one of the films on the previous page or use some of the items below to make up a new story!

Character	Plot hook	Location
Bobo the Clown	They have inherited an old mansion	The rainforest
Bam Stroker, Vampire	An almost perfect crime	A distant space colony
Valerie North, Politician	They found a bag with a million dollars	A small village in the 1800's
Jack Jax, Superstar Athlete	A science experiment has unintended consequences	An overcrowded metropolis
Samantha Shovel, Detective	An unlikely love story	A beach resort
Woofie the Wonder Dog	A family member has been kidnapped	A traveling circus

2. What will the movie poster look like?

Cast (*n.*): participants in a performance

The Devil's Debate

Choose one of the opinions below, and simply say whether you agree or disagree. Your partner(s) MUST take the opposite side.

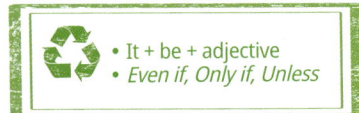
- It + be + adjective
- Even if, Only if, Unless

Example: It is acceptable for both men and women to stay at home and take care of children.

A: *I believe that it is perfectly acceptable for men to stay at home.*

B: *I disagree. Even if a man is good with children, it is really important that a mother be with her child when he or she is young.*

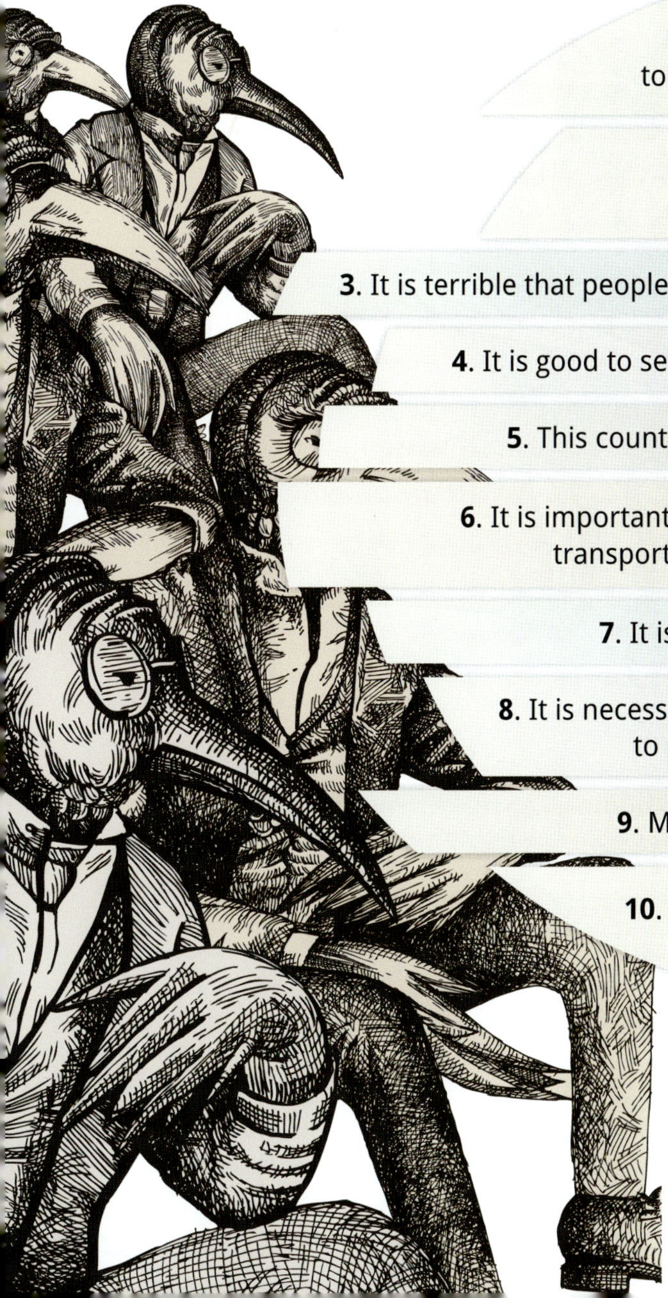

1. It is equally acceptable for men and women to stay home and take care of children.

2. English skills are more important than being able to speak your native language well.

3. It is terrible that people have plastic surgery for purely cosmetic reasons.

4. It is good to send children to study abroad during middle and high school.

5. This country would be better run by a woman than a man.

6. It is important that people give up their cars and use public transportation in order to help the environment.

7. It is improper to use cell phones in public places.

8. It is necessary that the government raises income tax by 20% in order to provide completely free education for everyone.

9. Money is the key to happiness.

10. It is important to follow what an elder says even if you disagree.

Basements & Lizards™

Create a character and take him or her on a quest unlike anything you have ever seen or heard before!

Part 1 ● Choose a hero from below and give him or her a name. Tell your partner or group your character's name, who you chose, and why.

_____ **the Bard**
Abilities: Can mimic any sound. Extremely handsome/beautiful
Flaws:
Items: Guitar

_____ **the Thief**
Abilities: Sneaking and Stealing
Flaws:
Items: Knife and Rope

_____ **the Warrior**
Abilities: Good fighter
Flaws:
Items: Sword and Armor

_____ **the Wizard**
Abilities: Can make things float
Flaws:
Items: Hat that can carry really large items

mimic (v.): to copy the sound of something

Part 2 ● Choose two extra abilities for your character. Be careful what you choose because each ability comes with a flaw. Tell your partner/group which abilities you chose and why.

Ability: Very brave	**Ability:** Can jump really high	**Ability:** Super smart	**Ability:** Doesn't feel pain
Flaw: Really shy	**Flaw:** Fear of heights	**Flaw:** Really boring	**Flaw:** Out of shape
Ability: Enhanced eyesight	**Ability:** Super fast	**Ability:** Can hold breath for long time	**Ability:** Born leader
Flaw: Afraid of the dark	**Flaw:** Extremely lazy	**Flaw:** Can't swim	**Flaw:** Gets lost easily
Ability: Excellent public speaker	**Ability:** Gets stronger from beer	**Ability:** Can speak to animals	**Ability:** Can heal injuries
Flaw: Terrible memory	**Flaw:** Gets angry when drinking	**Flaw:** Afraid of animals	**Flaw:** Hypochondriac

Choose an extra item that you think your character could use on the quest.

- Long pole
- Shiny red apple
- Perfume
- Torch
- Book of knowledge
- Hand mirror
- Raven
- Monster mask

hypochondriac *(n.)*: someone who is always worried about being sick

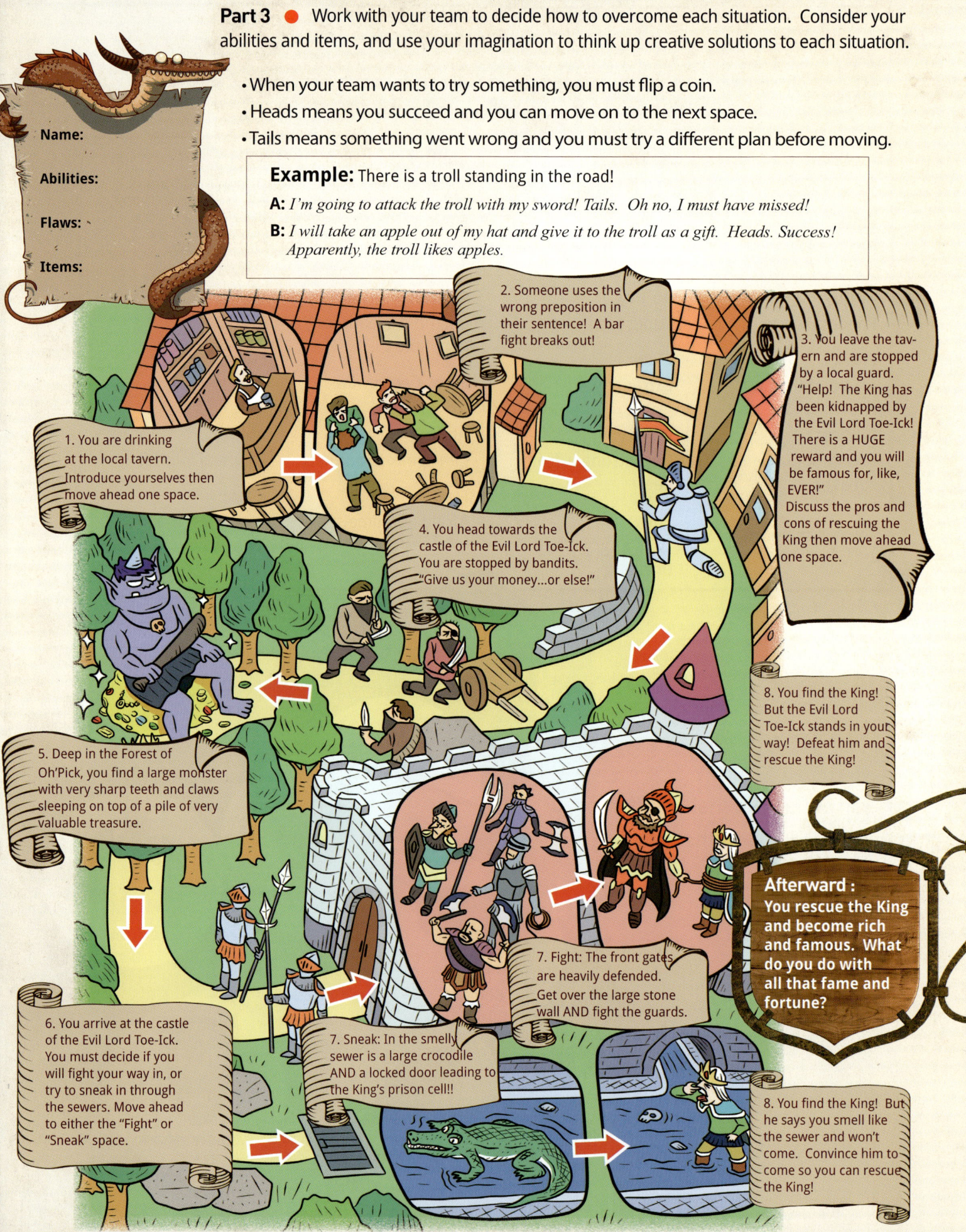

Bucket List

Looking at the list below, what are some of the things you wish to accomplish in your life?

- Which of these have you already accomplished?
- Which of these do you think you could easily accomplish if you put your mind to it?
- Which ones do you wish you could accomplish, but feel they're impossible? What are some ways of making them possible?

- ☐ Visit all the Wonders of the World
- ☐ Learn a new language
- ☐ Run a marathon
- ☐ Take up a new sport
- ☐ Ride a... (horse, camel, elephant, etc.)
- ☐ Resign from a job you don't like
- ☐ Start your own business
- ☐ Do something extreme (bungee jumping, skydiving, etc.)
- ☐ Climb a mountain
- ☐ Write a book
- ☐ Sing in front of an audience
- ☐ See the Northern Lights
- ☐ Visit Disney World
- ☐ Plant a tree and watch it grow
- ☐ Learn a new instrument
- ☐ Take up dancing
- ☐ Learn a martial art
- ☐ Live in a different country for at least six months
- ☐ Act in a film
- ☐ Walk the Great Wall of China
- ☐ Go swimming with dolphins
- ☐ Conquer your biggest fear
- ☐ Climb a volcano
- ☐ Fly in a helicopter
- ☐ Ride a rollercoaster
- ☐ See the Eiffel Tower
- ☐ Go on a cruise
- ☐ Fall in love
- ☐ See a castle in England
- ☐ Go on a safari

Activity : Haiku

A haiku is a poem with a very specific structure based on the number of syllables per line. A haiku is written in three lines: five syllables in the first line, seven syllables in the second line, and five syllables in the third line.

Traditionally, a haiku describes one specific moment or place. Though the poem is short, it can express a much larger situation or concept.

- What is your initial feeling from the poem?
- What adjectives would you use to describe it?
- What do you think has happened?

Example:
A simple letter,	5 syllables
Left alone beside the bed.	7 syllables
Fear has left it sealed.	5 syllables

Additional example:
A delicious cake
Is sitting on the table.
Then, Mr. Squiggles.

PART 1 ● Write Your Haiku
Given the structure above, practice writing your own haiku!

PART 2 • Haiku Factor™

Congratulations – you have been accepted as a top contestant on…Haiku Factor™!

The Rules of the Game: The Haiku Factor™ Host (who looks suspiciously like your instructor) will choose one of the images below. Each person or team will be given a few minutes to write a haiku related to that image. Once everyone has finished, you will present your haiku.

Your haiku will be judged by your peers or the Haiku Factor™ Host! They will give you your score and speak a little bit about how it made them feel.

Your haiku will be judged on the following criteria:
Creativity – how original and/or interesting
Style – how well it follows the form and idea of a haiku
Performance – how well you present your haiku

After several haikus are written, performed, and judged, the person or team with the highest total score is the winner of Haiku Factor™!

Haiku Factor Score Card
(All scores 1 to 5, 5 = best)

Creativity: __ __ __ __
Style: __ __ __ __
Performance: __ __ __ __

Total:

rhyme scheme *(n.)*: the pattern of rhyming lines in a poem

Additional Activities | 249